Children and Interculturality in Education

This book is unique in presenting new perspectives on how to introduce interculturality to children. It proposes critical ideas for introducing sensitive topics around culture, race and intersectionality. The book develops the reader's criticality and reflexivity, providing original and concrete tools to introduce interculturality to children and to make children aware of how intercultural issues matter in their lives and in the world at large. It includes case studies of children's realities from across the world, and provides insights into how to approach sensitive topics such as culturalism, discrimination, inequality and racism in relation to diversity in different contexts.

Written in the spirit of critical interculturality, the book will be of great interest to researchers and students in the field of intercultural studies, global childhood and early childhood education, as well as trainee teachers and educators.

Andreas Jacobsson is Senior Lecturer in Child and Youth Studies at the University of Gothenburg, Sweden.

Heidi Layne is Lecturer of Sustainable and Global Education at the University of Jyväskylä, Finland.

Fred Dervin is Professor of Multicultural Education at the University of Helsinki, Finland.

Children and Interculturality in Education

Andreas Jacobsson, Heidi Layne and Fred Dervin

LONDON AND NEW YORK

First published 2023
by Routledge
4 Park Square, Milton Park, Abingdon, Oxon OX14 4RN

and by Routledge
605 Third Avenue, New York, NY 10158

© 2023 Andreas Jacobsson, Heidi Layne and Fred Dervin

The right of Andreas Jacobsson, Heidi Layne and Fred Dervin to be identified as authors of this work has been asserted in accordance with sections 77 and 78 of the Copyright, Designs and Patents Act 1988.

All rights reserved. No part of this book may be reprinted or reproduced or utilised in any form or by any electronic, mechanical, or other means, now known or hereafter invented, including photocopying and recording, or in any information storage or retrieval system, without permission in writing from the publishers.

Trademark notice: Product or corporate names may be trademarks or registered trademarks, and are used only for identification and explanation without intent to infringe.

British Library Cataloguing-in-Publication Data
A catalogue record for this book is available from the British Library

ISBN: 978-1-032-24578-2 (hbk)
ISBN: 978-1-032-24579-9 (pbk)
ISBN: 978-1-003-27934-1 (ebk)

DOI: 10.4324/9781003279341

Typeset in Times New Roman
by Apex CoVantage, LLC

Contents

	List of figures	vi
	Introduction: Why children and interculturality?	1
1	**Every child is an interculturalist ... the problem is: *How to remain one?*** FRED DERVIN	10
2	**Interculturality and children: A global film and media perspective** ANDREAS JACOBSSON	51
3	**Interculturality, race and inequality in early years** HEIDI LAYNE	76
	Conclusion: Who are the real 'interculturalists'?	101
	Index	110

Figures

1.1	Knowledge of the World poster (China)	23
1.2	Representation of the Belt and Road Initiative	25
3.1	Examples of how pictures with Finnish words are used to support children who are learning the Finnish language for daily routines	83
3.2	Friendship tree (Ystävyyden puu). The word *friend* is translated in the languages of the children. Name tags with the names of the children are tagged to the tree for grouping purposes	85
3.3	Examples of self-made clothes for baby dolls from fabric donated by parents	86
3.4	Self-portrait of a young learner representing diversity	88

Introduction
Why children and interculturality?

'It wasn't this Mary!'

This is a book about children and interculturality. We find the topic intriguing for several different and intertwined reasons. Firstly, research on children and interculturality has until recently not been a particularly prioritized topic. With this book we thus provide a contribution to an important aspect of interculturality that deserves more critical scholarly attention. Secondly, children as a collective group have been, and to a certain extent still are (at least in some parts of the world), regarded as qualitatively different from adults. As such they are often deemed to be in need of special attention and care, as developing biological beings, and finally in the process of 'becoming' adults. This difference motivates a search for new analytical perspectives and new theoretical concepts to make sense of children and interculturality. Thirdly, the three of us all share a longstanding interest in a continuous critical rethinking and updating of the notion of interculturality in education.

The book focuses on interculturality and children, while arguing that this strand of research is beneficial to us all, 'adults' – in other words: while examining interculturality and children, we, scholars and educators, are made to *do, undo* and *redo* the notion for ourselves and others, learning *with* children in the process. In *Either/Or* (1843), a book about the conflict between aesthetic and ethics, the Danish philosopher S. Kierkegaard marvels at 'what native genius a small child often shows us a living image of the larger situation' (Kierkegaard, 2004, p. 32):

> How true to form human nature runs! With I was greatly amused today at little Ludvig. He sat in his little chair and looked about him with visible pleasure. Then the nanny, Mary, went through the room. 'Mary.' 'Yes, little Ludvig,' she answered with her usual friendliness and came over to him. He leaned his large head slightly to one side, fastened his

immense eyes upon her with a touch of roguishness, and then said quite phlegmatically: 'Not this Mary, it was the other Mary.' What do we older people do? We cry out to the whole world, and when it makes a friendly approach, we say: 'It wasn't this Mary.'

(Kierkegaard, 2004, p. 32)

Working on the highly complex and polysemic notion of interculturality, we also often exclaim that 'It wasn't this Mary' – referring to 'our' take on interculturality as being different and often better than our neighbours'. As such, interculturality often sounds like a magical word, brandished in different national and global educational contexts as a 'solution' to multifaceted societal problems (among others): 'dictatorship', inequality, nationalism, racism, social justice, stereotyping – all these being often understood in different ways around the world in both English and other languages. Using the notion of interculturality globally is equivalent to the hesitation of the blind monks in a Chinese saying trying to find out together what an elephant is, touching separately different parts of the animal: *is the elephant a rope, a wall, a tree, a spear* or *a snake?*

Commenting on what the blind monks are attempting to do one of Fred's students of intercultural communication education from China puts it nicely in the following quote:

> For most of us, our view on interculturality differs a lot. I also have some conflicting ideas with my partner when we talk to each other. But one thing is certain: we are all unable to understand comprehensively the connotation of 'interculturality'. All of us grew up in different environments, so for example the meaning of culture (which is central in inter-*cultur*-ality) in our hearts is not exactly the same. We are like those blind people who are telling what culture is through what we see and feel personally.

Another student uses an excerpt from the *Zhuangzi* (n.d.) to describe this conundrum that we all face: 夏虫不可以语于冰者，笃于时也, which can translate as *a summer insect cannot grasp the idea of ice since it knows nothing beyond its season.*

This is clearly evident in a call for journal articles that was launched by colleagues from Europe while we were writing this book. Focusing on the development of intercultural communicative competence (a central concept in intercultural scholarship), language learning and children under the age of 12 years old, the call is clearly anchored within very specific ideologies of interculturality. What we mean with *ideologies* here is simple: 'orders' to think and act in relation to interculturality in preferred ways from specific geo-economic-political contexts (see Dervin, 2022; Dervin & Jacobsson, 2022). As soon as one utters any definition, any objective and any expected outcome for interculturality, one falls within the scope of ideology, since such elements have to do with the way we have been made ('ordered'?) to think about self, other, groups, identities, inclusive/exclusive *modi operandi*, right/wrong, good/bad, etc. In the call, references are made to clear ideological takes on interculturality (among others): Byram's model of Intercultural Communicative Competence; The Reference Framework of Competences for Democratic Culture: Descriptors for Younger Learners; Intercultural Citizenship Education. These all derive from clear Eurocentric positions.

Our book is critical of such one-sided ideologies from one corner of the world. It represents a contribution to dispelling such obsessions in relation to children and to 'interculturalize interculturality' – a phrase Fred and Andreas (Dervin & Jacobsson, 2022) have used to urge interculturalists to see a bigger picture in the way they define, problematize and criticize the notion of interculturality, looking beyond their own corner (see Aman, 2018; Dervin & R'boul, 2022).

In what follows we strongly refrain from the all-too-common practice to impose interculturality from a specific perspective, may it be epistemological, methodological, or ideological perspectives – on children or anyone else for the matter. We have no intention to propagate and/or preach for a single 'true' definition or understanding of the notion, although we have our own preferences and ideological takes on interculturality (see Dervin, 2016, 2022; Jacobsson, 2017; Layne & Lipponen, 2014; Layne, 2019). Rather we propose that an open-minded, pluralistic and constantly changing conceptualization of interculturality is necessary to be able to capture some of the complexities of interculturality as an object of research and education for and with children. This includes the obligation to activate a critical awareness of our adult perspectives when we consider interculturality and children. Being alert to what this might entail in different situations and contexts, and in relation to research results and ideas that we are presenting in the different chapters of the book, is also essential.

What is a child? **Engaging with children in intercultural research and education**

Before we move further, it is necessary to clarify what we mean with the term *children* – or at least give the reader an approximation of the age groups that will be discussed in the book. Anyone can envision what a child is to them, but to present a clear-cut definition of general relevance is much harder to do. *Children* is a notoriously evasive concept capturing individuals from *newborns* to *adolescents* and, even, *young adults*. According to the UN Convention of the Rights of the Child (UNCRC) this includes everyone between 0 and 18 years. However, what constitutes a child differs from context to context and is connected to ideological, legal, religious and structural aspects in different societies (Montgomery, 2009, p. 3). One should also add the centrality of decisions about children made on the basis of financial and economic grounds. A common way of clarifying children is to negate them in relation to adults. Children are *non-adults*; they are young people in constant development and with different degrees of capabilities and competences. What is more, children define themselves as children and are regarded by adults as children (Rönnberg, 2003, p. 11). However, what this means for individual children is a completely different thing and is very much dependent on political, economic and ideological glocalized zeitgeists. For example, children can be *pampered* and *cared for* by parents, family and other caregivers until they are legal subjects in one context, and they can be *workers* and *earners* from an early age in another context. All *decisions* concerning children *can be made by adults* in one context and, in other contexts, children are left to *decide for themselves* (with all the words in italics here being potentially polysemic in these different contexts and in different languages, influenced by economy, local laws, welfare and [changing] traditions).

With this complexity and diversity of what a child could be, our book focuses on children from the age of 3–12, marking a kind of unprecise distinction between children and teenagers/adolescents. In the different chapters of the book, we will clarify what age groups that are specifically in question and problematize further how the notion of children is used if needed. Finally, adding another layer to the complexity, *childhood* is related to and overlapping with the notion of children, but it is not identical. Childhood is used as a framing of children's lives to help us talk about children's worlds in different contexts and times. We also note that childhood is a concept used for retrospective comparisons between generations from an adult perspective.

Going back to and contemplating a bit further why there is a lack of research on the topic of children and interculturality, we can imagine several potential reasons: 1) scholars of interculturality have to a large extent focused on 'larger' and 'adult' issues, such as (national) cultural differences; 2) the popular models of 'intercultural competence' – Byram's (1997) aforementioned model being one of them – are not adapted to children; 3) children are considered as not yet prepared for dealing with the complex and sensitive issues that are associated with interculturality; 4) there are other fields of study that are considered to have already produced this kind of knowledge, or at least a similar kind of knowledge, with a different terminology and other theories and methods; and 5) research on children and interculturality requires specific ethical consideration.

The fourth point is clearly relevant for us to take further into consideration. Looking at related fields of study can help us clarify some foundational points of departure for introducing interculturality to children. Developmental psychology and childhood studies represent two fields of study whose primary research objects are children and childhood/s. Both fields have produced influential research studies, from different perspectives, that have become common sense knowledge in (dominant) academia. The aim for developmental psychology has been, in a positivist manner, to 'identify universal patterns' of children's development (Hammersley, 2017, p. 117). Developmental psychology has had a strong impact on how children have been conceptualized in educational sciences in general and in early childhood education in particular – promoting the idea that children are going through specific stages of development. Contemporary research in developmental psychology has nuanced the biological positivist position and opened up for the impact of socio-cultural aspects on children's development and cultural variations in different contexts (e.g., Sommer, 2005).

Turning to childhood studies, this relatively new and interdisciplinary field has promoted – partly as a reaction to developmental psychology – a thorough social constructivist stance on childhood/s and children since the late 1990s (e.g., James & Prout, 1997; Prout, 2005). Childhood studies have been particularly important for activating an awareness of children's positions of dependence in *intergenerational* power structures and for promoting ideas on children's *agency* (Montgomery & Tatlow-Golden, 2018). Agency is a notion that captures children's own ability to create an understanding of their own lives and a potential to act 'upon their worlds, and to be competent and interactive members of society from birth' (Montgomery & Robb, 2018, p. 2).

Childhood studies has also implemented a cultural relativist position in relation to childhood/s when considered from a transnational and/or a global perspective, as an effect of the social constructivist stance permeating the field – but also since many researchers active in the field are coming from academic backgrounds in anthropology, education and sociology. Contemporary childhood studies acknowledge that childhood is a 'glocal' (local + global, Robertson, 1992) concept and that being a child and growing up differ between cultural and geopolitical contexts (e.g., Baraldi & Castro, 2020; Cregan & Cuthbert, 2014; Montgomery, 2009). Karen Wells (2021, p. 13) argues that an overarching aspect of contextual differences is economical: 'The task of a global perspective on childhood studies is to understand precisely how global political economy, and the structures it supports and the forces it mobilizes, reshape childhood in multiple spaces and times, societies and cultures'. However, diversity is of course not restricted to different cultures or different societies, all contexts are to some extent racialized, gendered and classed and because of this, 'the notion of childhood as having the possibility of being innocent, in the sense of existing outside of the symbolic and material nexus of political economy, has to be abandoned entirely' (Wells, 2021, p. 49). According to Wells (2021, p. 5) there is an unfortunate delay in childhood studies regarding taking seriously this glocal and multicultural complexity into consideration. Anglophone research is instead taking an unfortunate shortcut reproducing studies on middle-class children in limited geographical areas and extending their findings into generalized theoretical frameworks for understanding (global) childhood/s.

From this brief introduction to research on children and childhoods in other related fields of study we bring with us three notions that will be helpful for examining children and interculturality: 1) *bio-physical and psychological development* – children are undergoing a constant and individual process of development, gradually over time becoming more and more competent; 2) *agency*, children are active agents in their lives and not empty vessels waiting to be filled with knowledge by adults; children co-construct, resist and comply in different ways in different contexts; and 3) *intergenerational*, children are a group in society with a specific hierarchical position according to age. These ideas inform our book and provide a foundation for approaching the topic of children and interculturality in creative and stimulating ways.

Structure of the book and working method

'Is there a thought that would be worthy of not being thought again?'
Canetti (1989, p. 23)

All three authors are involved in teacher education in two Nordic countries: Finland (Fred and Heidi) and Sweden (Andreas). Andreas and Heidi have extensive experience of early childhood teacher education and of introducing issues of diversity and interculturality to pre-service preschool teachers. Fred is a novice regarding research and teaching on children and interculturality, however he is a renowned international expert on interculturality in education. Together we bring different expertise, knowledge and experience of teaching interculturality to this project.

The book is composed of three chapters, written separately by the authors but framed by a common introduction and conclusion where the content of the chapters is discussed, problematized and linked. In writing the book, each of us was responsible for one chapter, approaching the topic of interculturality and children as we wished and based on our own take on the notion. Regardless of our common background as researchers and teachers in Nordic teacher education, we also have different and sometimes divergent takes and ideas on the notion of interculturality. As we see it, in the same way as interculturality is a multifaceted and ideologically polysemous notion, a very important aspect of co-writing is to let differences 'seep' through the text – rather than to try to polish them away. These differences and sometimes conflicting ideas provide a basis for the reader to negotiate and dialogue with the distinctive voices in the book, and thereby help them develop their own thinking and opinion on the issues. It is fine to disagree around issues of interculturality, and it is something that we recommend the reader experiences too.

In the first chapter, Fred embarks on a personal, reflexive and academic journey, exploring the topic of interculturality and children, with modesty and humility. A particularly important part of this chapter is the presentation of actual voices from Chinese children interviewed by Fred and his colleagues on the topic of interculturality. The chapter also offers a useful review of international research on interculturality and children, from which issues concerning children and interculturality are drawn. Fred refrains from providing a (static) definition of interculturality in his chapter with the intention of questioning both the motives and the ideological practices behind definitions found in previous research.

In the second chapter, Andreas develops a critical discussion of what interculturality might be in relation to children, with the intent of using audio-visual media as empirical material for introducing interculturality to children. Since mediated interaction is becoming increasingly important in very young children's lives, it can be argued that it is a primary source of interculturality for children.

In the third and final chapter, based on her own extensive research on early childhood education in Finland and Singapore, Heidi presents two case studies on how interculturality is conceptualized in the different educational contexts. In her discussion Heidi problematizes interculturality in relation to inequality and clarifies how a narrow emphasis on language and cultural diversity is providing a fertile ground for structural racism among children, teachers and parents. Heidi also introduces pedagogical examples on how teachers can work with these sensitive issues together with children.

The three chapters and the concluding discussion based on the different approaches that we provide to the field are to be regarded as a first step on the way to problematizing interculturality and children in education. What this book does not wish to provide is a programmatic display of normative tips for introducing interculturality to children. Furthermore, the book does not aim to promote a specific interpretation of interculturality but to urge readers to 'interculturalize interculturality' (Dervin & Jacobsson, 2022) by opening up to other ways of engaging with the notion and, going back to Kierkegaard (2004), allowing ourselves to identify as many '*Marys*' as possible – in other words: interculturalities – in different corners of the world. This requires constant reflexivity and criticality from 'us' adults, learning *with* children and interculturality. Finally, and most importantly, our book does not serve as an exposé of *all children's worlds and cultures*.

References

Aman, R. (2018). *Decolonising intercultural education: Colonial differences, the geopolitics of knowledge, and inter-epistemic dialogue*. Routledge.

Baraldi, C., & Castro, L. (Eds.). (2020). *Global childhoods in international perspective: Universality, diversity, and inequalities*. Sage.

Byram, M. (1997). *Teaching and assessing intercultural communicative competence*. Multilingual Matters.

Canetti, E. (1989). *The secret heart of the clock*. Farrar, Straus, Giroux.

CoE (Council of Europe). (2020). *The reference framework of competences for democratic culture: Descriptors for younger learners*. Council of Europe Publications.

Convention on the rights of the child. (1989). Treaty no. 27531. United Nations Treaty Series, 1577, 3–178.

Cregan, K., & Cuthbert, D. (2014). *Global childhoods: Issues and debates*. Sage.

Dervin, F. (2016). *Interculturality in education: A theoretical and methodological toolbox*. London: Palgrave Macmillan. https://doi.org/10.1057/978-1-137-54544-2

Dervin, F. (2022). *Interculturality in fragments: A reflexive approach*. Springer.

Dervin, F., & Jacobsson, A. (2022). *Intercultural communication education: Broken realities and rebellious dreams*. Springer. https://doi.org/10.1007/978-981-19-1589-5

Dervin, F., & R'boul, H. (2022). *Through the looking-glass of interculturality: Autocritiques*. Springer.

Hammersley, M. (2017). Childhood studies: A sustainable paradigm? *Childhood, 24*(1), 113–127. https://doi.org/10.1177/0907568216631399

Jacobsson, A. (2017). Intercultural film: Fiction film as audiovisual documents of interculturality. *Journal of Intercultural Studies, 38*(1), 54–69. https://doi.org/10.1080/07256868.2017.1269061

James, A., & Prout, A. (1997). *Constructing and reconstructing childhood: Contemporary issues in the sociological study of childhood*. Falmer.

Kierkegaard, S. (2004). *Either/or. A fragment of life*. Penguins.

Layne, H. (2019). Ethnicity and race in childhood (Finland). *Bloomsbury Education and Childhood Studies*. (Digital resource). https://doi.org/10.5040/9781350934399.029

Layne, H., & Lipponen, L. (2014). Student teachers in the contact zone: Developing critical intercultural "teacherhood" in kindergarten teacher education. *Globalisation,*

Societies and Education, *14*(1), 110–126. https://doi.org/10.1080/14767724.201
4.980780
Montgomery, H. (2009). *An introduction to childhood: Anthropological perspectives on children's lives*. Wiley-Blackwell.
Montgomery, H., & Robb, M. (2018). Introduction. In H. Montgomery & M. Robb (Eds.), *Children and young people's worlds* (2nd ed., pp. 1–6). Policy Press.
Montgomery, H., & Tatlow-Golden, M. (2018). Reconciling childhood and youth studies and developmental psychology. In H. Montgomery & M. Robb (Eds.), *Children and young people's worlds* (2nd ed., pp. 7–23). Policy Press.
Prout, A. (2005). *The future of childhood: Towards the interdisciplinary study of children*. Routledge.
Robertson, R. (1992). *Globalization: Social theory and global culture*. Sage.
Rönnberg, M. (2003). *"Nya medier" – men samma gamla barnkultur? Om det tredje könets lek, lärande och motstånd via TV, video och datorspel*. Filmförlaget.
Sommer, D. (2005). *Barndomspsykologi: Utveckling i en förändrad värld* (2nd ed.). Stockholm: Liber.
Wells. K. (2021). *Childhood in a global perspective* (3rd ed.). Polity Press.
Zhuangzi. (n.d.). 庄子. https://ctext.org/zhuangzi/zhs

1 Every child is an interculturalist... the problem is How to remain one?

Fred Dervin

Warnings

The title of this chapter was inspired by how Pablo Picasso (in Hamer, 2019, p. 394) positioned himself toward art: 'Every child is an artist. The problem is how to remain an artist once he (sic) grows up.'

This first chapter is reflexive in nature and is meant to help the reader 'gather' their first thoughts about the topic of children and interculturality before they move on to the other chapters. The chapter is structured as follows: 1. I ponder over my own experiences of interacting with a few children in China and France; 2. I let you, dear reader, 'listen to' and reflect on research data collected about children's perceptions of intercultural issues in Chinese Inner Mongolia; 3. I review some of the literature published on children and interculturality in international journals. With all these aspects in mind, I aim to come back to the title of this chapter and propose a few elements to take away from my observations. This is to be considered as a journey that you the reader and myself embark on together.

A few words of warning before we enter the fascinating world of children and interculturality are needed. As a global expert on interculturality who has specialized in higher education and teacher education (e.g., Dervin, 2016, 2020, 2022) I am approaching the topic of interculturality and children with humility and modesty. Writing about 'children', speaking to readers from all over the world, I also need to be aware of my own position as a privileged white European scholar working in the Nordics, which necessarily limits my take on both *interculturality* and *children*.

First, I have had an uncountable number of opportunities to share my ideas and work through publications, lectures and keynotes around the world for the past twenty years, and I must remind myself constantly that thousands of scholars do not share the same privilege, their voices being often 'silenced' and 'violenced' by a system of scholarship which is overly Western-centric, white and English-based. My 'power' to talk must always

DOI: 10.4324/9781003279341-2

remind me to keep a low profile, be modest and listen to others with 'open ears'. So, my aim here is not to tell the reader what interculturality is or entails or how children should define and 'do' it. I need to silence my own ideological take on interculturality to think *with* you instead [I shall come back to this in a moment]. Finally, I am not entitled, as a white European male scholar (with potential symbolic academic power to speak for and over people from other parts of the world, which deserves to be disrupted) to determine what a child located in Atacama, Makassar or Rovaniemi, should learn for an object of research and education that is fluid, economic-politically embedded and so complex.

Second, I am about to speak of *children*. The word children can be troubling in the sense that it is a highly polysemic one. *When does childhood start and finish? Who decides?* When we say children, who do we refer to and from which part(s) of the world? Last year I asked a group of Chinese university students to define *a child* for me. We were doing this activity in English. After brainstorming together in groups for some minutes, they presented me with very similar definitions with the same age range and characteristics. I had noticed that only one of the groups had a reference on the notes that they had, to the UNESCO's definition of a child. I then asked all the groups how they had come to an agreement about their definitions and why they had picked a similar age range. They told me that they had checked how supranational institutions like the UNESCO had positioned themselves in relation to children. When I replied that I would have liked to hear more about how a child might be defined *in* (Mainland) China, they laughed and replied that they thought that I wanted to have a 'scientific', 'official' definition in English – hence the recourse to the UNESCO. Then ensued an interesting definition negotiated between them where people *disagreed about* what a child is in China and a precise age range. So, who is it that I refer to when I say *a child* in this chapter? If I am honest, I don't know, and I don't even think that I want to set an age range in stone. I know that in different parts of the world (and even within a country), a child can mean different things to different people and include different age ranges.[1] As you will see in the chapter, the previous studies that I refer to usually include children from 5 to 11; the examples I use from research data that I collected with a team in China revolve around children ages 7 to 11. These are age ranges that I include in the chapter.

Children's corner

My starting point is that, like any social being, children are also interculturalists, but maybe in *their-own-while-similar ways* as 'us' adults. I shall argue that working *on*, and maybe *with*, children and interculturality, requires us to step down from our pedestal as adults and to observe carefully what is happening in children's worlds [note the plural]. To explain the way that I will proceed in the chapter, let me venture a comparison with the French composer Claude Debussy (1862–1918). In 1908 Debussy published his six-movement suite for solo piano entitled *Children's Corner*. With this suite, Debussy wanted to capture the essence of childhood with charm, grace and humor, based on his relation and observations of his daughter Claude-Emma who was three when he wrote it. In *Children's Corner* he wanted to entertain the little girl by including her favorite toys and familiar landscapes while exploring music through what he perceived to be a child's world. The suite is not meant to be performed by children but by pianists to evoke childhood memories, fantasies and images. The first movement of Children's Corner depicts a young pianist practicing playfully key exercises, with the notes growing more and more complex, while indicating the boredom they experience while practicing. Another movement is about Claude-Emma's favorite toy, a stuffed elephant called Jumbo, needing a bedtime story before going to bed. *The Little Shepherd* piece creates a dreamy landscape for the little girl while *The snow is dancing* (often described as the most difficult piece to play) describes the experience of a snowstorm from a child's viewpoint. Inspired by this piece of music I argue that what we say and try to describe from children's experiences and takes on interculturality is based on our own imagination of what these could be, but that they do not necessarily represent 'their' reality. I also argue that children might not be able to play our own intercultural 'tunes' in the way we, as scholars, educators and decision-makers, intend it to be. In what follows, I am well aware that my discussions of interculturality and children are my own depictions of children's corners.

There have not been many children around me during my lifetime and I am experiencing some kind of impostor syndrome writing this chapter. As part of my teacher training in England I spent one week at a kindergarten observing and teaching a class – but I have no memory of that experience. I have 'met' friends' and colleagues' babies and children on some occasions but here again I do not remember much about who they were or what they did. All I remember is my own reactions and questions: *How do I communicate with these children? Which words can I (not) use with them? Is our interaction 'working'? Do they understand me? Do I understand them? How do they see me? Are they behaving and speaking with me the way they would speak and behave with others?*

Actually, if I try to dig deep into my memory, three very specific situations involving children where I felt unable to deal with what was happening between us, come back. Let me describe them 'naively' while sharing

Every child is an interculturalist ... the problem is 13

my own *very subjective* impressions of what happened. I will then discuss the way I present them.

- (China) I had met my friend's new-born baby many times within the last month. She had always been so excited to see me, smiling and laughing at the 'white man' enthusiastically [After rereading my chapter, Andreas wrote that the mention of the 'white man' is 'probably completely irrelevant from the newborn's perspective if you are white or not'. I come back to this later]. I had never known how to talk to her, since my Chinese is very limited and I assumed that she could not understand any language anyway. So, I spoke to her in whatever language that came to mind, not making full sentences and repeating what I found to be funny sounding words (e.g., 'baba-bebe'), making her laugh by pulling faces and so on. At that time, I had a two-month long beard, being too lazy to shave it. But one day I appeared at the door of their apartment freshly shaved. No one seemed to notice – or at least they did not mention it – except the baby. When she saw me, she started crying very loud, looking horrified when I approached her. Her mother tried to comfort her but every time I would show my face she would cry. I tried to calm her too and to take her in my arms, but nothing could stop her. On that specific occasion, I was unable to talk to her, to hold her or to make her laugh. *How to deal with this situation?* Obviously, she could not link up that freshly shaved white face with the funny bearded man of before. *Failure number 1.*[2]

- (France) I am sitting on a fast train from Paris to Nice, about to depart. The seat next to me is empty. Suddenly a family appears. They place a little boy (age?) next to me and ask in French if I can keep an eye on the child until the next station, where his grandparents were going to pick him up from the platform. Although I found it to be a very unusual request, I agreed. The next station was only 10 minutes away after all. The parents left. The little boy was sitting next to me with his toys on the table. I looked at him and started wondering how I could start a conversation to make him feel comfortable. I asked what his name was, how old he was. He whispered his answers which I couldn't hear very well. Then I took one of his toys and pretended that I was the toy, making a silly voice and noises. He laughed. The whole time I had these questions in my head: *am I speaking too quick? Am I using words that make sense to a child? Am I being boring and/or weird to him?* And ... *when are we reaching the next station?* There were many silences in our 'conversation' and I felt that the little boy was not interested in keeping it up. When I noticed that we were only a minute away from his stop, I told him to start packing up his toys. I stood up and took him downstairs to meet his grandparents. He ran toward them; they thanked me warmly and before I knew it, they disappeared, the boy never turning around to say thank you and/or goodbye. I remember feeling ashamed in that specific situation, ashamed of having failed at a 'conversation' with a child in a language that I had practiced since childhood myself. I had met thousands of people, from ministers to new undergraduates, rarely feeling anxious or unable to keep up a conversation or small talk. *Failure 2.*[3]

- (China again). I am on a hotel lift by myself. Suddenly the lift stops at another level, two children and their mum step in, pointing at me and whispering to the mum 'Mum, a laowei (a foreigner)'. I wave at them, saying a few words in Chinese, complementing the little girl on her beautiful dress. The mum then asks them to say something in English to me ('Nice to meet you. Where are you from?'). As I am about to answer, the lift stops and a service robot on its way to deliver food enters. The children then turn their attention to it, fiddling with its face and talking to it. I never had the opportunity to say where I was from. *Failure 3*.

What happened in these short narratives, which took place in two random social contexts and one with an acquaintance? Do these have to do with interculturality? At first sight they do: A 'foreigner' meeting children in two different countries. *But is it so simple?* The lift narrative could be clearly about interculturality, the trigger being children seeing my face and naming it as 'laowei' [one could wonder if their encounter with the robot was intercultural too?]. For the first and second narratives, it is hard to say how much interculturality has had an impact on the encounters. The first one appears to be about 'facial transformations' (beard/no beard), the same voice and attitude not helping to 'communicate', language being probably not an important factor here. If I had had a Chinese 'face', with or without a beard, would the same have happened? I can't say. The second narrative occurred in French. I felt uncomfortable and *failing* while sitting on the train with the little boy, having nothing to discuss or no real strategy to create 'togetherness'. But did he feel awkward? Did he care about what I perceive as a non-conversation and a failure? Did he just see me as an 'old boring grandpa'? Here again, I cannot tell.

My own take on interculturality – *listen to it, consider it but forget it* . . .

> 'Interpret nothing, explain nothing. Give those who want to rack their brains something to do.'
>
> (Canetti, 1989, p. 40)

Every child is an interculturalist . . . the problem is 15

This section represents some sort of a short break, a parenthesis before we continue exploring the topic of children and interculturality. Many readers, who may not be aware of my work, might be wondering about this 16-letter word that we are using repeatedly in this book: INTERCULTURALITY – *What is it? What is it meant to do? How am I supposed to use it?* What I want to do here is to 'come clean' about the notion of interculturality. I feel that I cannot continue using it without problematizing what I do with it in my own work and what I am planning to do with it in this chapter.

In my work, I view interculturality as both a polysemic and changing object of research and education. Having worked with colleagues from different countries, I noted that the way we define and 'order' people to 'do' interculturality in education can vary immensely across and even within borders. For some of us interculturality can be a mere synonym for *international* (i.e. people having crossed a national border); for others it can be about *language, race, ethnicity, Minzu* (in China), *indigeneity* and an intersection of other identity markers, such as *gender, capitals, status* and *age*. The use of the notion of interculturality is always embedded in broader economic-political-ideological stances, which makes it difficult for us researchers and educators to generalize about what it is and how we should 'do' it in proper ways for global audiences. *My interculturality is not necessarily your interculturality*, and I argue that no one has the right to judge other ways of seeing and 'doing' interculturality, giving too much power to their own take in the process (see Dervin, 2022). I believe that all perspectives on the notion are both 'good' and 'bad' in research and education and that we should be transparent about this vital aspect of scholarship on interculturality not to 'indoctrinate' people without them being aware of what they are told to think and do.

Let me take an example to illustrate my reticence at generalizing about the notion. Recently a friend of mine based in Shanghai sent me a picture of a poster presenting a kindergarten 'education philosophy' in both Chinese and English which listed the school motto, style of study and a certain number of school values. The poster is to be found outside the school, accompanied by pictures of children cooking together, doing sports, some of their calligraphy work, etc. Under the section called *Desired Vision* one can read: 'To represent Chinese culture globally and bridge international cultures locally'. I would argue that each word contained in this sentence is polysemic in English and that they could be understood in thousands of different ways in both Chinese and English and in different parts of the world. For instance, what *Chinese culture* and *international cultures* refer to is probably endless to billions of people. What to do with these (indirect) assertions about interculturality, seen in very similar utterances in most countries around the world, imposed top-down on children and parents, requires us to think further. We are faced here with ideologies of interculturality, which for Barker and Galasiński (2001, p. 65), '[. . .] can be understood as the attempt to fix meaning for specific purposes'.

Obviously, I have developed my own epistemic stance on the notion over the years – although I have changed many components in the process (see Dervin, 2016, 2022) – but I cannot assume that my take on the notion should be applicable for the billions of people who live on our planet. To be transparent about the way I see interculturality I feel that I need to share my ideological take on the notion at the time of writing this chapter. Andreas noted rightly that the 'components' that I list below are 'highly abstract and hard to grasp'. *Fair enough.* However, I repeat: *I am not here to give the reader a lecture about what interculturality is or is not, based on my own beliefs and economic-political ideologies.* I just want the reader to 'taste' some of my current ideas on this complex notion *for their information*. Some of the components listed below will appear 'nebulous' (which is fine, I consider myself the ideas of *tolerance, respect, democracy* and *social justice*, which are often used in research on interculturality, difficult to understand since they are used in somewhat meaningless and robotic ways), and I do recommend reading Dervin (2022) and/or Dervin and R'boul (2022) should the reader be interested in knowing more about the following elements.

I currently highlight three elements: *Change as foundation of interculturality; balancing proximity and distance with the other* and *ethics as an overarching principle of interculturality* (Dervin, 2022; Dervin & R'boul, 2022). These elements have been designed for scholars and educators to reflect on how they engage with the notion of interculturality.

Change as foundation

- Treat interculturality as perpetual co-change in yourself and the other
- Be at ease with change occurring in interculturality
- Accept and work from the incidental when interacting with others (beyond the illusion of encounters as 'programmed')
- Accept and navigate contradictions/consider both opposite and complementary in what we do with and say to each other in interculturality;

Balancing proximity and distance with the other

- Be unattached, take a bit of distance from things and people to gain a potential deeper understanding of interculturality
- Be proactive but prudent while interacting
- Acquire as much diverse knowledge as possible

- Listen to what you and others say (instead of merely 'hearing' self and other)
- Identify interconnections in likes and dislikes and what appears to be different and opposite;

Ethics as an overarching principle

- Practice introspection; reflect, unthink and rethink
- Practice integrity-moral (not use others, not be used by others; not fantasize about the other becoming you and vice versa)
- Be considerate (refrain from imposing own likes and dislikes)
- Push for harmony (balancing otherness with otherness, refuting sameness and not sacrificing some of your principles).

If I could summarize the three elements, I would maintain that they tell us that interculturality is about 1) balancing and reflecting upon the ways we speak and behave *with others*, and 2) both *observing* and *acting* upon the change that we experience in contact with each other. These elements are meant to clarify the *inter-* and *-ality* of the notion of *interculturality* – endless processes of transformations in the in-betweenness that we 'do' together with others. Note finally that there is no reference to the concept of *culture* in my take on the notion since, as I have argued for about 20 years, and in agreement with many other scholars from the 'West', I don't feel that this is the focus of interculturality – paradoxically since the concept is still contained in the notion (see Dervin, 2016). Culture is often used in an empty way (*what is it in the end?*) and as a substitute for other words that we may not wish to voice in specific contexts such as 'race', 'money' and/or 'development'.

At this stage in the chapter, you can read through the three aforementioned elements and think about the way you have engaged yourself with interculturality as individuals interested in interculturality and children, maybe as an educator, a scholar and/or a parent. Reflect on what these components mean to you and how they might relate to how you (have been made to) see interculturality with children. I will not engage further with these elements in the remainder of the chapter since my aim here is to explore 'freely' the topic of children and interculturality.

[Erase all this from your memory. Let's continue with children].

Trying to listen to children

When I told a couple of colleagues that we were working on this book, most of them said that this was too difficult, one even arguing that 'children are even more racist than adults'. This chapter represents one of the most daunting writing tasks of my career: my knowledge and experience of children are very limited and going back to the three short narratives about me 'meeting' children, one can see that I have problems in circumscribing them as 'intercultural' and determining if and how they functioned. Although I labelled them as 'failures', I cannot be sure how my young interlocutors perceived them [the boy on the train seemed to have other things on his mind – maybe he was excited to go meet his grandparents, maybe he was looking forward to getting a new toy, maybe he was just 'being in the moment'; my friend's daughter might have experienced fear of the unknown seeing me shaved, she might have simply not liked what she was seeing; the children on the lift shifted their attention quickly to some other (more exciting) stranger (a robot), attracted maybe by its lively voice, by the exciting music that it played, maybe they were under pressure from their mum to say something to me but were not interested in exchanging words with me . . .]. As a reminder, I am approaching the topic carefully, with *humility* as I said before, preferring to try to listen to children first and then to selected literature published in the English language in international journals. I am well aware that these cannot represent the complexity of interculturality and children as it is occurring globally on a daily basis. But I have to start somewhere to speculate about the topic. I am hoping to be able to share what I learned in the process and to confront my ideas with the observations I will make in what follows.

Where shall I start to get a sense of interculturality and children? I have already begun this process with myself trying to remember significant moments from my own experiences. I could have also tried to reflect on my own childhood – having navigated between different languages and countries as a child – but here again very little remains. As I was trying to scroll down my memories, I was reminded of de Saint-Exupery's (2015, p. 2) assertion in the *Little Prince*: 'All grown-ups were once children . . . but only few of them remember it' [maybe a first lesson for us scholars and educators working on interculturality and children]. A few (random) snapshots from my childhood: eating on the floor at my Iranian uncle's place, my small back hurting; visits to an uncle in Germany, whose home smelled of wood; being called a 'f*** bosch' by some other kids at school in Paris; asking one of my grandmothers to teach me some Polish (which she had forgotten, she claimed); hearing my class teacher telling my friend Habiba that she had a 'most peculiar smell'; etc. As I am listing these elements, I feel that they are so far away from me, as if they had not happened. For most of them I only remember a keyword, a smell, a feeling but they are so remote. For sure, these and many others that my memory has deleted or hidden have had an influence on my life, my career choices and my (changing) beliefs about interculturality. But as a child, from what I remember, I did not think so much about them. *They were just there, they were part of my childhood ecology.* Some of these events made me happy, sad and angry but I don't remember how I reacted to them or what they led me to say. I do have flashes in front of my eyes of how I discussed some of these events with my brother and my best friends but, parents and teachers did not seem to be involved in such conversations [is this something that I have removed from my memory?].

But enough with my *self* now, this won't lead us very far. Let me now turn to videos seen online. I will then examine in a non-systematic way research data that we collected with children about interculturality in China. I don't wish to comment too much on these snapshots of children's discourses. *I just want us to listen to and to 'taste' what children say.*

I did not find videos online that deal directly with interculturality and children. By this I mean, where children were asked upfront about how they see and experience certain aspects of interculturality. Bearing in mind what I asserted about the notion being polysemic and complex, I want to share two video excerpts from the magazine *Glamour* (2018, 2019) where people from ages 5 to 99 talk about 1. *What they find offensive* and 2. *What it means to be in love.* I will retain excepts from the videos based on what children between 5 and 11 say. This choice will appear random and, as a reminder, what a child is and when childhood starts and finishes are not universally agreed upon. I find the two issues presented in the Glamour videos (Glamour, 2018, 2019) to be relevant for interculturality:

What do you find offensive?

(age: 5) *when daddy yells at me*
(age: 6) *when someone pushes me*
(age: 7) *if people say bad words*
(age: 8, a black girl) *when people call me names*
(age: 9) *when people are rude*
(age: 10) *saying girls aren't strong*
(age: 11) *when people judge other people and that's very mean but they say* oh no offense *but it is still offensive.*

What does it mean to be in love?

(age: 5) *I play with them a lot*
(age: 6) *when people do special stuff for each other*
(age: 7) *to like somebody*
(age: 8) *when you really really like someone*

(age: 9) *I guess it is a mystery*
(age: 10) *to like someone and they like you and you like each other and you get married or something*
(age: 11) *when you really really like someone.*

I am not interested in some kind of gradation here – as in: the older the cleverer or the more interesting. At the same time, obviously, I do not intend to take these as representatives of the billions of children around the world. I need to remember that these were recorded in English, most likely in an English-speaking country (maybe the USA) and that the children appeared to be at ease with speaking in front of a camera. *Did they improvise or were they told to respond in a certain way?* I cannot tell. For the first question, we note that *offensive* for the interviewed children seems to have to do with speaking in certain ways (*yelling, bad words*), acting violently (*pushing*), saying something discriminatory and or/judgmental. Most of the ones reported as 'doing' these are called 'someone' or 'people' by the children – the other always seems to perform *offensive* in the quotes above. The question about love reveals two children answering the very same ('*when you really really like someone*'); the substitution of love with *like very much* (used as a synonym); playing and doing '*special stuff*'. Reciprocity from the other is indicated in about half of the assertions: *doing special stuff for each other; you like each other*; and maybe in *I play with them a lot*. The child age 9 is the only one to not define love, arguing that it is '*a mystery*'. These two questions – which might relate somehow to aspects of interculturality, *offense* and *love* – show that being offensive for these particular children is noticing certain (condemnable) formulations, words and actions in the other, while love is about *self* experiencing feelings for others, which might be reciprocal at times. There does not seem to be anything special to me here when compared to my own (limited) discursive perceptions of *offense* and *love*, except maybe the potential lack of self-reflection on how one can also be offensive to others (although this might be 'hiding' in some of the formulations such as *when people* . . . self might be there too but indirectly). If you can, try asking these questions to children around you and compare their answers to what we have just *listened to* here.

These were very short assertions from one small 'corner' of the world. Let us now listen to 15 children whom we interviewed in China about the global world. The children were between 7 and 10 years old, studied in a school located in the north of China. They were interviewed in Chinese in their school and I provide the translation of what they said. Choosing Chinese children is important here since their voices are not often heard in global research and in Western media. I thought that it would be interesting for the readers to listen to some of them engage with elements related to interculturality, to decenter potentially to another part of the world to explore what some children might think. With my research team from Minzu University of China (see, e.g., Yuan et al., 2020) in Beijing we asked the children how they understand the idea of internationalization, what they claim to know about the world *out there*, how they see themselves communicating with foreigners, and the languages that they would like to speak and why. I note that the Chinese word for *internationalization* (which can also mean *globalization*) used to speak to the students during the interviews was 国际化 (guójì huà). 国 translates as country, nation; 际, between and border; 化, change and transformation [literally: *change between countries*]. Interestingly, in Chinese, this last word shares the same final character as culture 文化 (Wénhuà), which indicates a process of change. While reading my chapter, Andreas noted rightly that children in Sweden might not understand the word *internationalization* without help from an adult. We could probably say the same about children in China. We could also probably claim that the questions asked to the children in what follows were far too difficult for them, in the sense that these aspects might not be part of their own interests in life. But let's see what they have to say.

Instead of commenting myself on what the children said to us, I am asking you questions to reflect on what you are *listening to* here so you can reflect for yourself instead of being guided by my own (potential mis-)interpretations. I also consider this to be an interesting intercultural exercise for the reader at this stage.

What meaning(s) do the children give to internationalization?

Interviewer:	Let me talk about a word first. Let's think about what this word means to you: internationalization. What does internationalization mean to you? Or what do you think of when you hear this word?
Child 1:	English.
Child 2:	China.
Child 3:	Japan.
Child 4:	I think that each country has its own language.
Child 5:	Every country has its own language.
Child 6:	I think that each country has its own way of communicating, language and various characteristics.
Child 7:	Internationalization aims to make our life better, to create peaceful things.
Child 8:	I think that internationalization means that our whole world can get along well and the whole world becomes very peaceful.

Child 9:	I think internationalization means that we should live a good life, and then eliminate evils. And then we live a good life like this.
Child 10:	I think that internationalization means beauty, peace and equality.
Child 11:	Internationalization takes place from a foreign country, it involves a lot of science and scientific knowledge brought by a foreign country.
Child 12:	It has something to do with advanced goods and inventions.
Child 13:	Internationalization brings some very scientific knowledge in foreign countries.
Child 14:	Internationalization is something more advanced and popular.
Child 15:	Internationalization is, maybe, what happens in our country.
Interviewer:	You mean what is happening in a foreign country?
Child 15:	Yes, show the strength of Chinese people on the international stage.

[There is a variety of answers in what the children say. While reading what they answered, what comes to mind? How do they position themselves, China and the rest of the world? Are you surprised by any of their answers? Are some of the elements that they put forward difficult for you to understand? What seems to influence the children in what they say about internationalization? Would children in your own context provide very similar answers? Finally, what might their answers tell us about what matters in 'their' world, their broader worldviews and their life expectations?]

What do the children claim to know about the world?

Interviewer:	Do you know anything about what is happening internationally? Can you give me some examples of what you are interested in?
Child 1:	Russia or some other country has a new president.
Child 2:	International affairs, such as this epidemic, China is the country that works hard to reduce the epidemic quickly, while other countries turn a blind eye to it. This is the first one. The second is that we Chinese have a characteristic that we all love our country. For example, Zhong Nanshan, the 'angel in white' [a Chinese pulmonologist who helped the country control the pandemic] gives us a lot of support. And helping poor girls in mountainous areas to go to college.
Child 3:	For example, Teachers' Day, National Day, Labor Day and Mid-Autumn Festival.

Every child is an interculturalist ... the problem is 23

Interviewer:	Aren't these all Chinese? Do you know some festivals from the rest of the world?
Child 3:	For example, Halloween is foreign, Christmas is also foreign.
Interviewer:	Well, besides festivals, their customs, what do they like to eat, do you know?
Child 3:	China or foreign countries?
Interviewer:	Foreign countries.
Child 3:	Foreign countries like to scare people and eat candy on Halloween. At Christmas the children make a wish and then Santa Claus will give them gifts from the roof.

[Russia often appears in the children's answers, as we shall see, most likely because they are located on the border to the country; later on, we'll also find many references to Japan]

[The data were collected at the end of 2021, in the middle of yet another wave of COVID-19, hence the reference to China's position in the world with the fight against the virus; one might feel either the voice of the Chinese media, parents and/or teachers in what child 2 is saying] [Reading Child 3's take on what they know about the world, what do you notice?]

(Figure 1.1 shows a poster found on the wall of one of the classrooms where the children were interviewed. It shows a list of countries and is

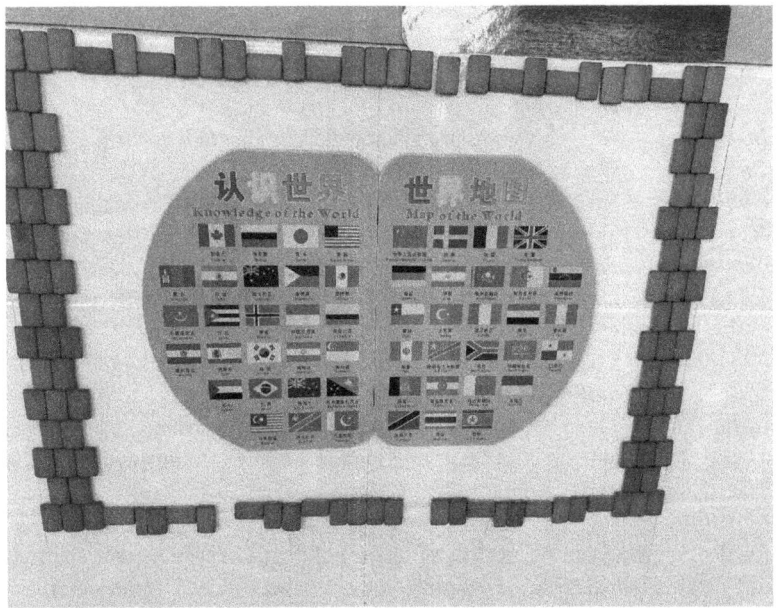

Figure 1.1 Knowledge of the World poster (China). Photo by author.

entitled in both Chinese and English *Map of the World* and *Knowledge of the World*. The poster seems to reveal China's take on the world, with top countries, partners and 'competitors' listed on top in this order: Canada, Russia, Japan, US, Sweden, France and the UK. Was there anything surprising for you here?)

What do the children want to know about the world?

Child 1:	I want to learn some Japanese language and mathematics learning methods.
Interviewer:	Why?
Child 1:	Because I heard that people in Japan have a high level of education. I want to know something about it.
Child 2:	I am interested in Trump
Interviewer:	You are interested in Trump. Are you interested in politics? What about you?
Child 3:	Uh, Ronaldo, Messi.
Child 4:	Well, I am interested in life.
Interviewer:	You are interested in life, such as life in which country?
Child 4:	The USA.
Interviewer:	Why?
Child 4:	Because there is a terrible epidemic there. I care about the situation there.
Child 5:	I like Andersen from Denmark. I like his fairy tales or stories.
Child 6:	Hawking. And Hillary.
Child 7:	Music.
Interviewer:	Ah, which country's songs do you like to listen to?
Child 8:	Black Pink from Korea.
Child 9:	I would like to know more about Japan.
Interviewer:	Why?
Child 9:	Every time the teacher says that Japan is very good.
Child 10:	I want to know about the traditional culture of different countries in the world.
Child 11:	I want to learn about the future economic development of the world and the future economic trend of China.
Child 12:	I want to learn six languages, because learning six languages can facilitate communication between countries and speak about global warming.

[Reflect on the main figures found in the children's answers: what are their positions? Countries? And why might they have been picked by the children?]

[Which answers would be similar in your own context? Would they be argued for/formulated differently?]

Every child is an interculturalist... the problem is 25

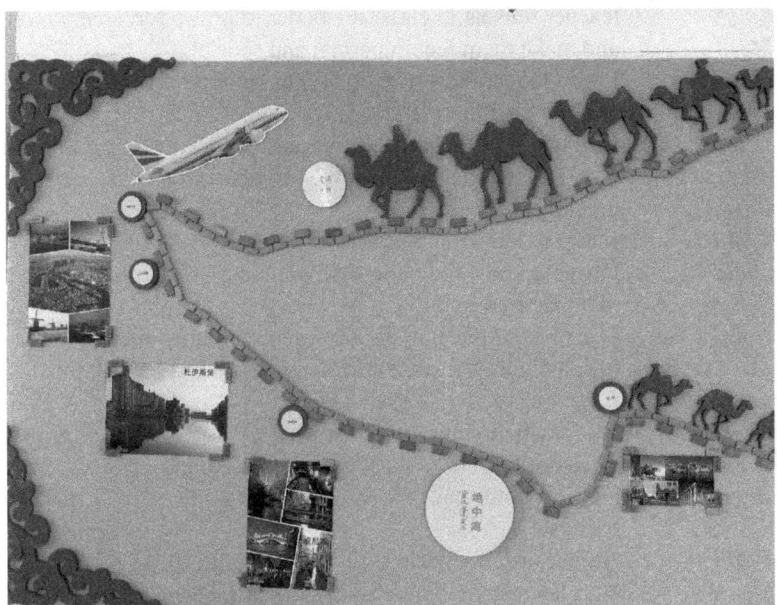

Figure 1.2 Representation of the Belt and Road Initiative. Photo by author.

[Speculate again on who might have influenced the children in answering the way they do].

[Figure 1.2 is a representation of China's contemporary take on the Silk Road (renamed the Belt and Road Initiative) that was pictured in one of the classrooms we visited. The Initiative has 138 member-countries, with 38 countries in Sub-Saharan Africa, 25 countries in East Asia and Pacific and 18 countries in the European Union. Although Belt and Road 'countries' are often mentioned in the Chinese media and education as strategic partners, none of the children referred to the Initiative or its members. Why might it be so?]

How would the children deal with talking to a foreigner?

Interviewer:	Do you think that if you had a foreign friend, maybe from Japan or other countries, would you be ready to communicate with them?
Child 1:	I'm introverted. I don't like to talk. I don't want to communicate with him, and I don't have enough ability.
Interviewer:	What preparations would you need to make to communicate with a foreigner?

Child 2:	To speak their language and praise them more is what our teacher tells us in class. It's better to praise foreigners more and make them feel important and special.
Child 3:	I need to learn to say hello to him, to make friends, and then to remember their language.
Child 4:	I am ready to speak to them because we have learned English now, if we go to England, we can generally know the basic greetings.
Child 5:	I need to know their taboos and to learn their language.
Child 6:	I need to know their etiquette, what they like to eat and what they like to watch.
Interviewer:	So, for example, there is a German standing here who wants to chat with you, what do you think you need to ask him?
Child 7:	How are you, Sir? Say hello first.
Interviewer:	Yes, say hello first. And then what?
Child 7:	Then ask him what about the story of Hitler.
Interviewer:	Do you think you are ready to communicate with foreign friends?
Child 8:	No because my basic skills are not solid, I can't speak foreign languages. For example, when I go to a convenience store, I can't understand English.
Child 9:	Chinese is ready, but nothing else.

[The themes of language skills and knowing about foreign cultures (taboos, etiquettes) seem to dominate the children's answers, and thus do not seem to deviate from 'standard' answers one might get from both children and adults around the world. However, some of the answers might appear quite special: reflect on them, trying to imagine why the children might have provided such answers.]

What language would the children want to learn?

Child 1:	Japanese.
Child 2:	English.
Interviewer:	Why would you want to study Japanese?
Child 3:	Because I usually watch Japanese cartoons with translations, if I learn Japanese, I don't need to read Chinese translations.
Interviewer:	Why do you want to learn English?
Child 4:	Because I want to go to the United States, I feel it is very modern there.
Child 5:	I want to learn Portuguese because they play football well.
Child 6:	Italian because Italians like to cook, and spaghetti.

Child 7:	Russian language because it is a fighting nation.
Child 8:	I want to learn Korean because the Korean Black Pink is there.
Child 9:	I want to go to America to study English.
Child 10:	Be careful you won't get shot.
Child 9:	But life there is very good, it feels very free.
Child 11:	I want to study English and Japanese. English is the universal language in the world. Now it's also used in the textbooks. It's also used in studying abroad. For Japanese: Because I like the customs and food there.
Interviewer:	What language do you want to learn?
Child 12:	Arabic.
Interviewer:	Why Arabic?
Child 12:	I want to go there by camel.
Interviewer:	Can't we get a camel in Inner Mongolia?
Child 12:	Yes.
Child 13:	I want to learn Japanese so I can go to Mount Fuji and buy a Volkswagen.
Interviewer:	Volkswagen can also be bought in China.
Child 14:	Italian and French, because France is more economically developed.

[Here again, the children provide a variety of answers about the languages they would want to learn and why. Try to map out the geopolitics of their answers: What patterns seem to appear? Can you speculate again why Chinese children would provide these answers and what it tells us about the worldviews they are constructing?]

Do foreigners know China?

[Three children were asked to reflect further on what they think 'foreigners' know about China today. What might these excerpts tell us about how politics and ideology influence[4] the children's thinking here? Does anything surprise you in what they maintain here, considering China's position in the world today?].

Interviewer:	Do you think that foreigners have a deep understanding of our China? Is the China they know the real China?
Child 1:	No. For example, when they take Chinese cultural relics to foreign countries, China still spends a lot of money to buy them. I don't know how important this thing is to China.
Child 2:	I think it's okay. Today, China's economic development is very good. Prices are cheaper than foreign countries. Compared

	with foreign countries, China has advantages. For example, some countries are dissatisfied with the rapid development of our country. They are jealous and suppressed us.
Child 3:	They don't have a deep understanding. They not only don't understand our China, but they also spread rumors. For foreigners who discredit China, I would like to tell them that explaining China's current development is not what foreign media say.

This third entry into interculturality and children (following my narratives and the *Glamour* videos), using a small amount of interview data with Chinese children points at a certain number of interesting elements:

- Internationalization seems to be problematized by the children as something both positive (e.g., access to development, entertainment, peace) and negative (e.g., misinformation about China, historical trauma);
- Discourses of modernity, economic and technological development accompany discussions of the US, Japan and some European countries – and China;
- References to global entertainment and famous figures are made;
- Children's geopolitical location might influence how they speak of intercultural issues (e.g., closeness to Russia and Japan);
- The children all seem to recognize and understand the importance of using another language (not their own) to communicate with someone from another country [I am not sure if this is a universally accepted point];
- 'Evils' from the past seem to be used to discuss interculturality [history as an important component];
- The voice of the teacher seems to influence how they talk about members of other national communities (e.g., 'Japan is very good');
- Politics and the media seem to be heard in what some of the children say about China and other countries, leading to some Sinocentric statements;
- Similar discourses about the importance of cultural knowledge (taboos, festivals, foods) are found as in the discourses of adults in many other contexts.

Although my own narratives were about 'real encounters' with children, what this section has shared with us is children's voices about their perceptions of topics related to interculturality. I now feel the need to dig deeper into children's direct and indirect intercultural experiences and encounters.

My next source of inspiration is research *per se*, hoping to find more about this topic.

What can we learn from the literature?

In this section I am curious to find out about previous research on interculturality and children. I focus here only on research published in English in some international journals between 2013–2021, being very much aware of the fact that these studies are limited when one considers how complex the topic is globally. I proceeded by reading as many papers as I could on interculturality and children. Using the keyword *intercultural/ity* limited the kinds of papers that I retrieved since other notions such as *multicultural, culturally-responsive* and *global* might be used by some researchers in many parts of the world. My goal here was not to present an exhaustive picture of the kinds of research being done in English but to get a 'taste' of some of the voices on the topic.

Without much surprise most of the research that I identified in top international journals was related to education. I note that most papers considered interculturality from the perspective of the international (different countries), with some focusing on issues of racial encounters locally. In the end, I retained about twelve papers that introduce a variety of perspectives and topics. The following contexts are covered: *Australia, Belgium, Finland, France/Germany, the Netherlands, Spain, Tunisia, the UK* and *the US*. My first reaction was similar to when I read research on university students: researchers tend to start from a preferred ideological take on interculturality ('scientific' but also 'economic-political') when they examine how children behave and/or discuss intercultural issues. The clear Western-centrism of approaches, theories and methods in the papers was also something that I am accustomed to in my work in higher education.

Children's knowledge about the world: *What and how?*

Let us start with a paper published by Scoffham (2019) in the field of geography education: *The world in their heads: Children's ideas about other nations, peoples and cultures*. Based on a review of research in the UK and 'Westernised industrial countries' since the 1960s, the paper provides answers to four questions, which I covered partially in the previous part: 'What do children know about different nations, people and cultures? What are children's feelings toward different nations, people and cultures? How do children develop their ideas about the wider world? What are the implications for classroom practice?' (Scoffham, 2019, p. 90). The author starts by reminding us that there has been a lot of previous research on how children conceptualize *countries*. However what Scoffham is interested in is how children construct their ideas about the other – rather than just what they know.

Scoffham (2019) presents and discusses two ways data concerning interculturality and children have been collected: asking them to name countries (with differences noted between different age groups, older children being able to name more 'real' countries than younger children who focus on both real and imaginary countries) and drawing free-recall maps of countries (here again with differences between age groups whereby older children appear to be more able to represent/draw less dislocated maps of the world).

These are the main elements that Scoffham (2019) finds from his review and that are relevant to us here:

- Age, gender, ethnicity and social group membership seem to influence the children in their knowledge of the other;
- There is 'extraordinary growth in world knowledge' (2019, p. 89) in middle childhood, with stages in naming or mapping the other having been described;
- Conceptualizing what constitutes a country is usually challenging for children;
- Learning about other countries does not necessarily make children more open-minded about them;
- The role of parents, peers and family, travel and (social) media is noted in influencing ideas and attitudes;
- Direct encounters with the other seem to leave a long lasting positive/negative impression on children;
- There tends to be a lack of awareness of the Global South among children from Western industrialized countries and the legacy of colonialism still seems to dominate views on certain parts of the world;
- Learning about the other in school can create strong emotions in children, question their identity and be related and/or lead to negative or positive positioning toward other countries (for example, if a country is a former 'enemy').

Based on these elements, Scoffham (2019) proposes the following recommendations for working on interculturality in school. *First* the author suggests moving away from the 'overtly factual' since, he argues, such knowledge is 'fraught with difficulties' (Scoffham, 2019, p. 97), forcing teachers to make clear-cut decisions about what to include and exclude, often reflecting specific values and priorities – I would say 'ideologies' – and thus fragmenting and simplifying the complexity of the world. *Second* the author recommends taking into account the emotional in introducing the other in the classroom. Based on his review, Scoffham (2019, p. 98) also suggests that 'teaching programmes which are predicated on powerful emotional experiences may be just as or even more effective than those which focus on knowledge transfer'. Teachers should take into account the potential aforementioned stages in children's knowledge about the world (e.g., locational knowledge), from infant egocentrism to more expansive modes of thought, when introducing them to the world and interculturality.

Children and interculturality in schools: *Pulling the rabbit out of his hat*

The work of Oakleigh Welply (2018) reveals another aspect of interculturality and children which I have not discussed but only hinted at until now: *discrimination*. Welply (2018) examined implicit discrimination toward a specific group of children (10–11 years old) in a culturally diverse primary school in the East of England (Muslim children). The author starts her paper by reminding us that many previous publications have 'widely documented' prejudice, stereotyping and discrimination among children, with violence, racist acts and exclusion being common forms. She also reminds us of the strong influence of wider social and political discourses on children's attitudes toward the other. Using the concept of micro-aggressions as a starting point, she focuses on the 'othered', whose experiences differ from many other children, and describes Muslim children's experiences of implicit discrimination in interactions with peers at school. Using group interviews including different kinds of children Welply (2018) found that the children's position toward the place of the other was largely ethnocentric. She notes (Welply, 2018, p. 377):

> These representations were underpinned by tacit forms of stereotyping and discrimination towards Muslim children, located at the intersection of race, religion, language and national identity. These negative views were in turn internalised in Muslim children's discourses of difference.

The following discursive elements, at the intersection of race, religion, language, nationality and immigrant status (among others), were found in what the majority (white) children asserted: *essentializing segregation* whereby race, skin color and religion form 'natural' borders between people; the use of *discursive buffers* such as 'I am not being racist/offensive but' (after uttering something racist, see similar remark in one of the Glamour videos), which turns the blame on the other for being too sensitive and thus problematic; *stereotyping and attribution* (use of certain derogatory terms to refer to a language).

Welply (2018) deplores the contradictions between her findings and the constructed school ethos of tolerance and multiculturalism, which might confuse the children even more – *tolerance* for some children urged them to argue that they were 'not being offensive' when they uttered something which could pass as racist. The large influence of wider historical, global and local discourses was also clear in the data that Welply collected. For example, the fact that Muslim and non-Muslim children lived in different parts of the same city seemed to contribute to discriminatory discourses – a vision of the other from a distance (Welply, 2018).

[I was surprised by Welply's research results as I found very similar results as with older youths and adults. Her framework is that of Critical Race Theory and I wondered how much this focus guided the study toward the results that she had identified – and missed out on other perspectives with children. I was also reminded of the specific context of the study ('multicultural England' with specific ideological takes) which had a clear influence on how the children seemed to engage with otherness. This reminds us of the importance of being reflexive and critical of the ideological positions that we take on interculturality in research and education and to ponder over the potential influences they might have on different aspects of our research and educational initiatives].

Teaching children interculturality: the use of story and picture books

With this section we enter the realm of introducing children to interculturality in educational contexts. I have identified tens of papers focusing on the use of picture books to do so – which is not surprising considering the importance of picture books for children. In what follows I review a certain number of these papers from the Netherlands, Spain and the USA.

The first paper, published by Tomé-Fernández et al. (2019), looks into values and intercultural experiences through a didactic practice based on two picture books in the Spanish context. Having asked children age 9–10 about the contents of the books, they found that the children were able to engage with positive values such as *helpfulness, friendship* and *empathy* while reflecting on the stories and characters. At the same time, the authors note that prejudices were dismantled and that positive intercultural experiences took place in the school as a consequence.

This is how one of the picture books used by the authors is presented in the paper:

> In *Mariama, Diferente Pero Igual*, everything is new to Mariama. After a long journey from Africa, she begins to discover new languages and

customs. With the help of her new friends, she makes an effort to learn the language and discovers that the only difference between them is their skin color. One of the most representative quotes from the book is 'They were children who did not have to worry about anything else but being children' (Cornelles, 2014, n.p.; our translation), which reflects on the complexity of the protagonist's childhood.
(Tomé-Fernández et al., 2019, p. 208).

The authors worked with the children by adopting the read-aloud method, pausing from time to time to ask them questions and to observe the pictures with them (e.g., 'When does the sentence "For Mariama, all was new" appear in the book, and what exactly does it mean?', Tomé-Fernández et al., 2019, p. 208). The authors report that the read-aloud led to debates among the children and to dig deeper into the subject by other questions being asked. All in all, the children appeared to be aware of the book characters' difficulties as migrants (language, communication, negative feelings) and of the 'culture shocks' that they might experience. As a conclusion to their study, the authors propose a 5-stage method for including such picture books in teaching interculturality: *preparation* (looking for proper books reflecting the diversity of the classroom); *recognition* (dramatized read-aloud leading to children's first reactions and questions); *deepening* (role play, debate); *critical level* (investigation on the book characters); *social development* (link the didactic initiative to values in the classroom) (Tomé-Fernández et al., 2019, p. 212).

The second study that I would like to present focuses on folktales (de Bruijn, 2019) beyond reification and simplification of 'target cultures', proposing children's intercultural participation as a working principle, which the author describes as 'it is exactly in the multiplicity and diversity of children's transactions with folktales that we can find the greatest intercultural educational potential of these materials' (2019, p. 319). Using data collected at a Dutch kindergarten and with second grade children (ages 5–8) de Bruijn (2019) shows how children from diverse backgrounds interpret folktales through different lenses. Having organized reading groups with the children, the author aims to 'study how children's literature can stimulate children's cultural literacy within ethnically, religiously and socio-economically diverse classrooms without favoring or excluding one specific group of children right from the start' (de Bruijn, 2019, p. 321). One of the stories included in the research project is entitled *Djoha Rescues the Moon from the Well* and is described as follows:

Djoha and his donkey Babori are on their way home when Djoha is shocked to see that the moon has fallen into a well. He wants to save the moon from drowning and put it back where it belongs: among the stars in the evening sky. Djoha throws one end of a rope into the well and tells the moon to hold on tight. Of course, when Djoha starts pulling on his end of the rope, the rope comes loose from the edge of the well and Djoha falls down. Lying on his back, he sees the moon in the sky above and feels very proud of his heroic deed

(de Bruijn, 2019, p. 323).

One of the most important and strongest aspects of the study is to take into account the children's active role in meaning-making processes. Although the children were from diverse backgrounds, they were not considered as engaging with the stories as mere sources of knowledge of specific cultures.

The context of the next two papers appears to be the USA but the authors are not explicit about it. In 2015 Iwai published the article entitled *Using multicultural children's literature to teach diverse perspectives*. Like most papers on interculturality and children the author starts by stating the importance for teachers to take diversity into account in their classroom. For the author using children's literature can help both teachers and children to learn about their differences and similarities; support them in questioning their 'negative stereotyping'; foster their awareness of diversity (and of their own). Iwai (2015, p. 82) also provides five 'tips' for using multicultural literature: (1) *model positive attitudes toward diversity* (teachers show that they care about all students and treat them equally); (2) *select high-quality multicultural children's books* (teachers should pay attention to use a variety of genres from poetry to comics; images contained in the books; make sure that dialogues are as authentic as possible and that words in foreign languages are spelled correctly; people are portrayed as individuals – not mere representatives of a 'culture'); (3) *plan effective instruction and set a concrete and relevant purpose, prompting the children to develop their thinking and awareness*; (4) *use multicultural children's books across the curriculum*; and (5) *partner with the community* by inviting guests from outside the school context. In the fourth set of advice, the author (2015, p. 85) suggests the following concrete activities with children, which can be adapted depending on the age:

- *Open-Mind Portraits*. Students illustrate a character's face from a story and write the character's feelings and thoughts.
- *Double-Entry Journals*. Students write quotes from the story in the left column and reflections on the quotes in the right column.
- *Storyboards*. Students select important events from the story and illustrate the sequence of those events in graphic organizers.

In a similar vein, in her 2018 paper, Esteves also describes how children could be introduced to global perspectives through the use of picture books. The author highlights perspectives that overlap with the previous paper, focusing on the importance of working with similarities and differences in order to combat 'us and them' and of developing empathy for the other. Working with picture books can also encourage questions 'and spurs a design to learn *more*' (Esteves, 2018, p. 73) and to develop critical thinking. Putting forward a list of activities, the author proposes to:

- work on children's personal cultural identities and the development of beliefs about themselves and others (e.g., consider one's name in relation to the dominant culture while examining the names of characters in a book);
- consider but also move beyond the five Fs of food, flags, festivals, famous people and folklore (reflecting instead on how one's 'culture' might look different and be perceived by an outsider);
- look into heritage and family history (Esteves, 2018, p. 75): 'Consider asking students to trace their family's roots and record their countries of origin on a map. What countries are represented? What areas are not represented? What is going on in those parts of the world today?').

For the five Fs, the author (Esteves, 2018, p. 74) recommends working on these questions with children to develop their reflexivity around interculturality (again, depending on their age, adaptation is needed):

- Why should we learn about different ways of life around the world?
- Why is it important to understand your own culture and the cultures of those who live near you?
- How might life be different for you if you were born somewhere else?
- What seems strange or exotic about cultural practices in the books?
- What may seem strange about where you live to other people from around the world?
- How does your way of life impact other people from different parts of the world?

Esteves (2018, pp. 75–77) ends by making specific book recommendations, which I will not detail here. However, I note that Esteves categorizes the books as follows: *Books that celebrate the world's people; books that celebrate places;* and *books that promote curiosity, peace and social justice.* As aforementioned, it is important to be as inclusive as possible and I would suggest including books in languages that the children don't know for them to explore with the teachers (with a focus on sounds, letters if possible and pictures).

The last paper of interest concerning the use of children's literature for interculturality is more specific than the previous ones and relates to Welply's (2018) aforementioned paper. It also reminds us of the importance to introduce topics that may not always be 'rosy' with children. In the paper, published in 2018, Newstreet, Sarker and Shearer explain how to use literature text sets to teach empathy, especially to address Islamophobia beyond opposing 'Christians' vs. 'Muslims'. The context of the study is the USA, and the children were of (mostly) Hispanic heritage. The project also led to a pen pal exchange with students in Bangladesh. The teacher used texts related to refugees in the USA, without specifying their ethnicity. The authors note that the work they did around the books empowered some of the students to talk and write about their own experiences of coming to the USA. By using multiple text sets the authors were able to provide the children with 'opportunities for intertextuality while reading, fostering text-to-self, text-to-text, and text-to-world connections (Keene & Zimmerman, 1997). Students make connections between current and previously examined texts (including multimedia presentations), constructing new understandings about complex topics' (Newstreet et al., 2018, p. 562). Like previous authors, Newstreet et al. (2018) suggest a range of activities to be adopted with children around picture books. These include 'predicting from photographs', whereby paintings and/or photos of assorted experiences of Muslims people from around the world are presented and discussed with the children, with an aim to help them grasp the complexity of 'being a Muslim' today (Newstreet et al., 2018).

Trying to make a difference for interculturality and children

In this section on previous research I am particularly interested in other kinds of approaches that attempt promoting specific aspects of interculturality. These include here: foreign language learning-teaching; enquiry-based global curriculum; world cultures curriculum; and telecollaboration.

In a rare paper from outside the West, *Any role for foreign languages in promoting children's critical thinking? The case of stereotyping*, Ben Maad (2020) focuses on potential change in early-years stereotyping by means of an 'awakening to languages' intervention in the Tunisian context (see also Auger & Le Pichon-Vorstman, 2021). *Awakening to languages* here refers to exposing monolingual children to foreign languages, not to teach them different languages but to try out sounds, experiencing things in these languages and reflecting back on their own language. Working with six-/

seven-year old speakers of Tunisian Arabic, the author had the children discover and compare languages such as Berber, French, Hindi and Mandarin, playing games, preparing food, designing and dressing in different clothes (Ben Maad, 2020). The author shows that attitudinal change did occur in the children after the various activities, turning cultural absolutes into variations in their perceptions of the other.

Engaging children with global issues through an enquiry-based global curriculum has been another way of introducing and examining interculturality among children. In a 2019 paper, Acevedo worked with such an approach with kindergarten children in the USA, focusing on knowledge, perspective and action as indicative of intercultural understanding. The scholar's entry point is children's playful interactions. Starting from the idea that children in learning contexts should be considered as 'problem-posers, problem-solvers and creators of knowledge' (Acevedo, 2019, p. 381), an action research took place and is described as follows:

> The theme *Diversity within Unity* supported shared and individual enquiries around local and global cultural communities. The global curriculum used literature as windows into multiple worlds and encouraged play as experience. Cultural artefacts were also explored in order to provide access to cultural spaces, stories and experiences.

The results of the study show that

- *intercultural understanding as knowledge* shifted from both local to global and global to local; the children also integrated new vocabulary from other 'cultures' into their play;
- *intercultural understanding as perspective* (e.g., open-mindedness, developing empathy) was evidenced, with steps toward anticipating complexity being taken by some children, feeling the need to make sense of global experiences rather than assume based on own experiences and perspectives and be inclined to empathize with others;
- *intercultural understanding as action* urged the children to listen to each other, change their interpretation and think together with others.

Heidi J. Torres's work is also of great interest here. In a 2019 paper, she explores the outcomes of an elementary world cultures curriculum for 8–9 years old in the USA. The author understands culture as 'a framework that describes and makes visible the different ways of believing, understanding, valuing, and feeling that social groups develop and express through a variety of visual, aural, written, or oral media' (Torres, 2019, p. 549) and focuses exclusively on 'national cultures', admitting to the potential contested nature of the term, which, however, she finds fitting for working with children. Torres (2019, p. 553) also admits that one cannot develop an approach to interculturality and children that could take into account the diversities of factors that impact how children think and experience this phenomenon. However, she decided to focus on one aspect that the literature has consistently been discussing in the West: 'a way for children to begin cultivating intercultural competence is to move beyond negative, stereotypical beliefs and attitudes as described in cultural cognition research' (Torres, 2019, p. 552). Having designed a curriculum on world cultures through a global education focus (duration: 11 weeks), the author introduced the children to these topics: *people's geographic places in the world, cultural universals, surface and internal culture, cultural similarities and differences*. Engagement with artifacts, texts, video and performance strengthened their acquaintance with these topics. Individuals from outside the school context also supported the teacher by making presentations in class and guided her in selecting topics of interest. Here is an example of a sequence prepared by 'Korean consultants' (Torres, 2019, p. 558):

> Korean consultants designed a full simulation of traveling to Korea, including departure from the airport on 'Korean Airlines,' Korean food and part of a movie 'on board,' and arrival in 'Seoul'. Once in 'Seoul' – a classroom set up as different sites in the city – students were able to visit various places, including a school where they learned about the Korean alphabet and practiced writing, a Korean home where a consultant talked with students about cultural norms and shared materials found in a typical home, and a clothing shop where students were able to try on traditional Korean attire.

According to the author, the children showed positive development of intercultural competence to varying degrees and the children's ability to engage with complex ideas around cultures. Comparing the children's cultural understanding prior to the course and after, more robust and complex understanding of culture (e.g., recognition of internal culture, similarities and differences) occurred; as well as developing resistance to stereotyping; attitudinal shifts (nascent open-mindedness, movement toward perspective taking and developing empathy). Torres (2019, p. 566) provides the following example:

> Dallas, in explaining the importance of learning about other cultures, gave a rationale for perspective taking: 'If they would know other people's perspectives and what they might think, it would help us understand each other better.' In this comment, he exhibited an understanding

of the importance of knowing other's perspectives, a significant step in developing cross-cultural awareness. Dallas further understood the importance of asking questions in order to access another person's perspective and not make assumptions based on one's own point of view. When meeting someone new from another culture, Dallas said he would ask questions so 'you don't come up with any bad biases about other people, like, "Oh, he probably doesn't speak English, so he's not going to understand anything we say."'

Evaluating the experiment, the author also reminds us of the importance to replicate and test it in other contexts since what may work in a specifically situated pedagogic initiative, involving a specific teacher, may not work in other contexts (Torres, 2019, p. 570).

The last paper adopts a different perspective by focusing on a story and drawing exchange, named 'intercultural Storycrafting', during which 10–11-year old children created a shared narrative culture with a geographically distant group (Belgium/Finland). This powerful paper starts from the important argument that interculturality is not something that can be learned through acquiring a skill set but by learning to create shared understandings within and across communities, giving the children a voice in deciding what counts as 'culture' – while recognizing that their voice is not fully separated from that of adults. The authors, Piipponen and Karlsson (2021), show how children negotiated shared understandings in a third space, the meaningfulness of aesthetic experiences in intercultural exchanges between children in terms of emotions, senses and imagination and how narrativity, creativity and communality engaged children in encountering. As such, their interest is in the processes rather than products of interculturality. This is how the storycrafting method used is described by the authors (Piipponen and Karlsson (2021, p. 4):

> *Tell me a story, any story you want. I will write it down exactly like you tell it. When the story is finished, I will read it out to you and you can make any changes or corrections* (Karlsson, 2013). The stories were told as a class, as a small group or individually. Either the teacher or a classmate would scribe. (. . .) The teacher would then read the partner class's story or sometimes several stories aloud to the children, first in the school language and then in the original language. After that, the children drew a picture of the partner class's story, and told their own stories to send back to the partner group. For each drawing, the class teacher prompted the child to 'tell me about this drawing' and the child's words were noted down.

Children 'doing' interculturality outside the school context

I have managed to identify a certain number of studies about initiatives urging children to engage with interculturality outside the school context, often directly in contact with the other.

In *Intercultural non-formal education: what the children think*, Młynarczuk-Sokołowska (2022) listens to how children (ages: 7–12) with different socio-economic and ethnic backgrounds, perceive non-formal education activities carried out by Polish non-governmental organizations (NGOs) dealing with culture and art, integration and social activation, and human rights. The activities included workshops, multifaceted educational projects and competitions. The author (2022, p. 83) details how the children engaged in discussions of psychophysical human functioning, economic and social status, cultural diversity of the local environment and country of residence, and cultural specificity of selected areas and countries after the activities. This is how two children who took part in a workshop describe what they experienced (Młynarczuk-Sokołowska, 2022, p. 89):

> (. . .) I really liked the way we worked in groups, because everyone had different ideas, and from these different ideas one good thing could be created. Sitting on the carpet, we were collecting ideas for the creation of works.
>
> (. . .) For example, Miss brought us a backpack and there was something written in Chechen that we didn't understand and she said she had found it in our school. And it was mysterious, but I like things like that.

Młynarczuk-Sokołowska (2022, p. 95) concludes that non-formal intercultural education is beneficial for children and that its active learning character seems to help develop specific aspects of children's intercultural competences such as empathy.

In a similar vein, Melin and Wagner (2015) describe the impacts of primary school exchange programs between France and Germany and the learning opportunities of such intercultural encounters. The authors observed the children in their everyday school situations when meeting each other in their respective contexts, focus on rich spontaneous moments of play and self-portrayal. Since the children did not share a common language, they had to deal with communicative challenges by using strategies such as mediating with objects and animals, body-related expressions, teaching each other in the process (e.g., through mimetic learning). The scholars note that activities organized and managed by the teachers differed in the sense that the children did not need to take so many initiatives and test different strategies compared to spontaneous encounters with their peers (Melin & Wagner, 2015). This could suggest the need for children to be placed in active positions as actors – without being told what to do – in intercultural encounters.

The following two papers all deal with telecollaboration between children (age 5–6) located in different parts of the world. Set in early childhood education Magos et al.'s (2013) paper linked up children from rural Greece with children in other parts of Europe (e.g., Bulgaria, Romania, Poland) online. During the exchanges, the children described their lifestyle, family life, school community, exchanged fairytales, stories, photographs, drawings etc., with others and were able to view their own culture from a distance, according to the authors. The teacher served as a mediator and decisions about content were systematically negotiated with the children. The children's languages were used and translated by the teachers into English for others to translate into local languages. Here is a description of one of the exchange cycles:

> The first cycle of action-research aimed at the development of a first acquaintance and communication among the Greek students and their peers from other countries. Children's faces and names, school grounds as well as the villages or cities where they lived were the main topics of intercultural exchange in the first cycle (Magos et al., 2013, p. 368).

The researchers note that the children were first and foremost interested in the similarities between themselves and their partners when they saw their pictures, claiming at times that they looked like them, had the same hair color, etc. (Magos et al., 2013, p. 369). The children also discussed linguistic diversity, trying to engage with pronouncing names and letters, again focusing on similarities (for example by noticing the presence of a similar letter in names). The use of fairytales was also fruitful as a way of urging the children to think about similarities and differences between them (e.g., Snow White). Some of the topics that were introduced to partners also triggered important discussions around moving and migrating to get a job – a phenomenon the Greek children were aware of in their village. At the end of the project when the children were interviewed, they expressed their strong interest in continuing working with their European partners. For instance, one of them said: 'I am going to tell the next year teacher: Madam, I want us to continue being friends with the little children from the computer.' (Magos et al., 2013, p. 371).

The second and last paper discusses a similar initiative between Australian and Korean children (ages: 10–11). Over a two-year period, Walton (2019) studied online classroom exchanges which took place between the children through Zoom encounters based on question-and-answer games and PPT presentations. The author notes that the Australian children (who were the focus of this paper) made efforts to think more specifically and critically about race and culture by interacting with their Korean peers, although some of their comments were, at times, racist. Walton (2019, pp. 275–276) argues, however, that children need to be encouraged to be critically reflexive about what they say and think when engaging with the other. Discussions of race often make teachers uncomfortable in the classroom but there is a need to both confront and reflect on this aspect of interculturality.

What to take away from (limited) personal and research experiences, as well as previous studies on interculturality and children?

> 'Children aren't coloring books. You don't get to fill them with your favorite colors.'
>
> (Hosseini, 2010, p. 42)

After rereading what I have written until now, and to my surprise, I would say that what I found is neither overwhelming nor incomparable to my previous engagement with the field of interculturality in education. The topic is obviously not an easy one and as I was reading through the literature, I felt sometimes uneasy and started wondering if what some of the researchers were doing was too simplistic in the sense that they seemed to replicate what 'we' have done with adults. The expected interculturality of looking into children that I wished to experience – some kind of *dépaysement* – was not as strong as I thought it would be. Yet we need to be careful here and avoid rejoicing. Although I shared anecdotal experiences from China and some research data with children from the Middle Kingdom, most of my observations and the identified literature are but from one 'children's corner' of the world (borrowing Debussy's piano suite title used in the introduction to this chapter). As such they are still very adult-centric and Western-centric, which represents a major issue. When observing children 'discoursing' and/or 'doing' interculturality through our own economic-politically tainted eyes, can we do 'real' justice to their 'own' sense of interculturality? [while rereading this question, I am wondering why I used 'own'. Did I mean that children have specific ways of engaging with interculturality as a group and/ or as individuals?]. In a book based on long-term open dialogues with Chinese university students about interculturality a colleague and I (Dervin & Tan, 2022), we noticed that the students tended first to 'mimic' and 'parrot' our own takes on the notion as well as what their former teachers and textbooks had 'ordered' them to believe in [Tournebise (2012) had noted the same with Finnish university students of interculturality, who also rehearsed ideologies passed onto them by their professors, in what resembled *intercultural indoctrination* versus *intercultural communication education*]. With more critical engagement with our discourses, daring to draw on their own diverse experiences, the Chinese students started to open up and to challenge our arguments and to speak about interculturality in different ways. If young adults can be indoctrinated and misled so easily by unreflexive and 'pushy' scholars' and educators' ideologies, why would children be different? The questions I had in mind constantly while reading the literature were: *Who is really talking in what scholars are making children say? What do the children really think? Do they really care about what they are being asked? Does this all make sense to them?* The idiom 鸡同鸭讲 in Chinese means *chicken and duck talk*, which can be translated as *talking at cross purposes* or *being unable to communicate with each other*. Is this what we experience (without realizing) when we 'chickens' (scholars, educators, adults . . .) speak to 'ducks' (children) about interculturality? If there is one thing that I take away from reflecting on interculturality and children, I would say that this is the most important aspect: we really need to take the time to listen to children – as much as we need to listen to diverse adult voices – to avoid misconstruing their (complex) views and experiences when we put words onto 'their' interculturality. Speaking and listening to children from around the world (and not just a selected range of European countries) should be a priority before we continue engaging with the topic. This is an important intercultural challenge in itself.

Reading through the literature, here are the most important elements that we need to either take into account or continue exploring in research and education.

What do we seem to know about interculturality and children but still need to question and explore?

- Children are definitely *interculturalists*: from day one, they learn to interact with the diversity of the world *every minute* [diversities within family; (simple and complex) representations of glocal diversities in social (social) media, books . . . ; diversities on the streets, in stores; diversities in schools . . .]. I have witnessed for instance how the Chinese baby whom I mentioned at the beginning of this chapter could easily transition from one person to another within and outside her extended family – with each member being a diversity in themselves, with their own ways of speaking to her, of holding her, of playing with her, and even of annoying her. The world is also around her at all times: she has English words on her clothes; she drinks milk from Germany; she hears TV series from South Korea blasting from her aunt's phone; she is surrounded by American brands; etc. This 'basic' introduction to glocal sociality and humanity for a baby will continue lifelong and, at some point, they will come across a person who might speak a language that they do not necessarily understand, a person who follows a specific religion . . . Scholars mention repeatedly that children become aware of 'cultural', 'racial' and 'ethnic' discourses when young; they can develop 'stereotypes', 'misconceptions', 'prejudices', 'racist discourses' in early childhood. I use inverted commas for all these terms here because they are rarely defined in the studies I consulted, generalized to *children*, forgetting that different parts of the world either avoid using some of these terms or understand them in so many different ways, which tends to empty them of universally agreed-upon definitions. In all the papers that I consulted, it is clear that the scholars are very much influenced by glocal discourses and ideologies of interculturality. If their research were replicated in other parts of the world, I am not convinced that they would 'do' it the same way, in similar terms, with similar outcomes and recommendations. For example, the idea that children are 'aware of culture at an early age' could mean thousands of different things to people globally – and even within the same geopolitical sphere. We thus need to engage with these 'problems' further with children and (why not?) propose new terms to describe what, *as children*, they experience, 'do', think globally in their daily engagement with interculturality. 'Their' world is not separated from 'our' world, however, like 'ours' 'their' world is plural, embedded in global capitalist zeitgeists and worldviews, which impact 'our' and 'their' life experiences. Yet, I am calling for scholars and educators to develop a specific language to refer more specifically to 'their' realities [why not ask children themselves to 'name' these realities, not caring too much if they can't and/or don't want to?].

- In a similar vein, most research has attempted to identify stages in children being more positively disposed toward 'culture', 'race' . . . and their attitudes becoming more negative toward in-groups and out-groups. *But interculturality is an unstable lifelong process for which we can never be ready*. On some occasions some children might actually be better at interculturality than 'us'. The same children might not be so good at it in completely different contexts and with different people [in the same way we adults fail and succeed at interculturality in a non-linear way]. *How to collect such data when we know that what we say about self and other is always embedded in specific contexts and with specific people? How to collect such data when children – like adults – might find it difficult to 'do' and 'speak' about such a changeable and potentially unnerving phenomenon as interculturality? Do we always say what we mean in interculturality and do we always 'do' it successfully as adults ourselves? Finally, considering the very diversity of children around the world (language, gender, worldview, economic status, lifestyle . . .), how could such stages be universally applied?* We know that depending on the (perceived) freedom that we have in a given interaction what we dare to say about ourselves and others might vary. I suppose that, for children, such pressure can be different and some might not have developed a sense of 'sociality' in certain situations and speak their minds (as in: 'Mum, why is this man so tall?' in front of a stranger in a shop). However, like adults, children do develop a sense of interaction, of performing, of protecting their face, politeness, (white) lies, etc. This also means that what children might say and do when asked to say and do by adults, is the result of co-constructions. As a fragmentary and spontaneous phenomenon, interculturality requires from us to find ways to capture it that are flexible and reflexive of its own non-linearity. Children around the world will experience it as such, will co-change with it and we need to listen to the contradictions, instabilities, mistakes that they go through, not to 'order' them neatly but to observe simply the complexities of the notion as experienced by them as children. We also need to accept *for* them and *with* them that they will fail at it too . . . No one will ever be 'perfect' at interculturality. No one can say what 'good' interculturality is to the whole world. So why might anyone wish children to learn or to respond to it like *super-persons* (see *The Reference Framework of Competences for Democratic Culture: Descriptors for Younger Learners*, for children age 10 years old and beyond, CoE, 2020)? Children should be left to face these contradictions, to live with them and to reimagine the world and others as they wish, without us telling them how to conceptualize interculturality, often in weak ways (see Welply's, 2018 very convincing critiques of 'tolerance-speak' in British schools).

- One aspect of the studies that I consulted which I found to be important (but probably not surprising) is the clear influence that schools, (text)books, (social) media, parents, fiction and, at times, travel and contact with others have on children. The short review of data collected in China had already given us a hint at this (and I believe that readers struggled at times to understand what the children were saying because of their lack of acquaintance with the context of their assertions). Bearing in mind these multifaceted influences (for which we are all partly responsible: one could say that *there is a part of us adults in every child*) thus remains essential when discussing interculturality with children. Helping them identify these influences in them, questioning the way they are formulated, weighing their pros and cons, comparing them to the children's own life experiences represent interesting ways to engage children in applying a bit of 'discourse detergent' (Barthes, 1994, p. 122) to allow them to think, unthink and rethink for themselves. I must confess that I was somehow irritated by some of the studies that I consulted, which tended to 'judge' and 'attack' some of the children they were researching about the stereotypes they held. As a reminder: *'their' stereotypes often derive from 'our' own stereotypes*. What is more, since stereotypes cannot be 'removed' as such (we all have them inside of us, even when we claim that we don't have any stereotype. This very claim could be seen as a stereotype. *I have no stereotype is a stereotype*), why expect children to 'destroy' them when they are fed with them all the time through 'our' media, the education we build for them, the politics that 'orders' them in-/directly to be and think in specific ways . . . ? There is an interesting contradiction to be dug into here. I am convinced that instead of 'censoring' stereotypes or 'punishing'/'criticizing' children for using them, helping them to reflect on their origins (without always being able to identify them) is a deeper reflexive exercise that could become an important way of thinking in them [*why do I think what I think? Who has 'ordered' me to think this way? Why am I imitating this way of behaving in front of the other? How the way I formulate what I think reflects such influences? How could I unthink my thoughts? . . .*]. Observing and guiding (unstably) children to analyze constant back-and-forths between themselves and their environment could be a powerful tool to rethink interculturality *ad infinitum*. This pushes us scholars and educators as well as children to 'think away' from interculturality-as-a-phenomenon to interculturality-as-a-polysemic-and-complex-human-and-societal-object.

- Since children are themselves interculturalists who experience the notion as they see fit and/or under our influence, I do believe that we might want to focus on their expertise to learn more about interculturality ourselves. At the end of this chapter, I am not convinced that we adults are better experts at it. As I said at the beginning of this chapter, many of my friends and colleagues warned me against writing on children and interculturality, with many giving me the impression that they looked down on children, as if they did not know anything about the topic, considering them as the 'dummies of interculturality'. I was reminded here of how, as a child, my grandparents systematically asked me to be quiet when I wanted to take part in their conversations about politics since, as they said, I was *only* a child and had nothing to contribute to these conversations [I had noticed that this argument was very convenient when I questioned their beliefs and ideologies]. I would also urge us to let children question our own views on how we see and 'do' interculturality: let them criticize us, 'order' us to behave differently and to reconsider our thoughts in playful ways. More importantly: let us look into the mirror of interculturality that children might reflect – in their own complex ways and experiences. I do believe that we will definitely learn a lot (at least) about ourselves . . . *What can I learn from and with interculturality and children?* could be the question guiding us in our engagement with the notion of interculturality.

I dreaded writing this chapter. Writing about interculturality and children was an intercultural process in itself. As Dostoyevsky (2014, p. 59) put it however: 'The soul is healed by being with children.' I feel refreshed and full of hope in front of the exciting ideas that emerged from engaging with this aspect of interculturality of which I was unaware. Obviously, I need to remind myself of the dangers of romanticizing children here [considering the state of the world and the failures of interculturality that we are witnessing as I am writing this, there is a danger of hiding in a 'rosy vision' of children]. Yet I am convinced that we can learn a lot *from* and *with* children. As intercultural 'specialists' themselves, they seem to experience the notion in ways that we do not always allow ourselves to experience as adults. Interculturality is a phenomenon – like all social and human phenomena – which pushes us in all directions, making us lose our bearings, experiencing contradictions, re-positionings, instabilities, pains, joys, etc. – which we often try to 'correct' or 'fake' *in front of* and *with* others. Since the 1950s interculturality has been problematized by means of *objectivity* (often under falsely critical subjectivity-preferred perspectives), *rationality* (culture, identity, race, but also non-essentialism which is, by the end of the day, an indirect reminder that we must be rational) and *scientificity* (e.g., Western models of intercultural competence; data analysis, which rarely admits defeat). Children are clearly torn apart between different poles when engaging with interculturality, which they seem to be somewhat comfortable with, unless adults 'order' them to run away from one of these poles:

- their own imaginary and creative ways of engaging with the realities of the world;
- their questioning the unquestionable and wish/joy to contradict, provoke, play;
- the concrete complexities and pressure of meeting another person which lead to multifaceted co-change (a stranger or a family member);

- the influences of the adult world in all its intricacies (in a random order: capitalism, rationality, social media, ideologies, tendencies to indoctrinate and mold).

Reflecting on these elements, my only wish at the end of the chapter is for us adults to continue engaging with the important question found in the title of this chapter, which I now remodel: *How could we remain children as interculturalists with our own and shared unstable and contradictory ways when we grow up?*

Notes

1. In one of my courses, a student wrote about the word *teenager* in Chinese: "We usually refer to a teenager as someone between the ages of 13 and 19, using the word 青少年 (qing shao nian). But when we talk about *youth*, 青年 (qing nian) or 少年 (shao nian), very similar concepts to *adolescence*, which refer to people between the ages of 15 and 34".
2. Andreas notes about my use of the word 'failure' here: "I'm not sure *failure* is the right word in relation to these short stories. It could be more adult experience of lacking proper resources for handling a situation. This is interesting in relation to interculturality which often leads to similar experiences". I come back to this use later but I would like to maintain that the very word 'failure' was chosen for the following reasons: The word tends to be avoided in relation to interculturality since we are often made to think that we should not 'fail' with the other and I have insisted in my work that we must consider failure as an important part of 'doing' interculturality since, I argue, we can learn from failing (Dervin, 2016). The obsession with *success* could lead us to *mere performing, pretending* and *faking being together, respecting each other* and *being tolerant* of what we say and do [all these expected results of interculturality, put forward by many scholars of interculturality, are polysemous and would deserve to be unpacked multilingually. For instance, what *tolerant* means to me can be very different from how readers or even my co-authors might define the idea of tolerance]. What is more, since I am not used to interacting with children, for me, the encounters described here are first and foremost *intercultural* – not in the sense that they are 'international' but related to encounters between strangers who need to negotiate their interactions, their ways of speaking and behaving, their representations of each other. My take on interculturality here is one-sided (as will be discussed later) since I cannot tell how the children perceived our communication.
3. Here, Andreas asserted while engaging with my chapter: "This is clearly not a failure, rather a common experience when interacting with children. They do not necessarily react in an adult way. Instead of a failure it is an experience of communicating with a child that you do not know".
4. Andreas reacted to my use of the verb *influence* in my questions to you the reader: "You use the idea of 'influencing' children a couple of times in the chapter. As a reader it seems that you state that children are doing what adults expect of them and do not have a voice of their own. This connects to the ongoing scholarly discussion on children and agency". In this section, I use the verb *influence* in questions directed at someone else, which means that I do not necessarily believe that there are such influences. I am sure that many of you will not see such

influences. However, you might also want to reflect on the important discussion of children's agency mentioned by Andreas: Pay attention to the use of this verb in the rest of the chapter and how it is modified (as in '*seems* to influence') or not and what this might reveal about the way I indirectly position myself in relation to the burning issue of children's agency at different points in the chapter (and in the rest of the book – we'll come back to this point in the conclusion).

References

Acevedo, M. V. (2019). Young children playing their way into intercultural understanding. *Journal of Early Childhood Literacy, 19*(3), 375–398. https://doi.org/10.1177/1468798417727134

Auger, N., & Le Pichon-Vorstman, E. (2021). *Défis et richesses des classes multilingues: Construire des ponts entre les cultures*. ESF Sciences Humaines.

Barker, C., & Galasiński, D. (2001). *Cultural studies and discourse analysis: A dialogue on language and identity*. Sage.

Ben Maad, M. R. (2020). Any role for foreign languages in promoting children's critical thinking? The case of stereotyping. *Language Awareness, 29*(1), 60–77. https://doi.org/10.1080/09658416.2019.1686508

Canetti, E. (1989). *The secret heart of the clock*. Farrar, Straus, Giroux.

CoE (Council of Europe). (2020). *The reference framework of competences for democratic culture: Descriptors for younger learners*. Council of Europe Publications.

de Bruijn, A. (2019). From representation to participation: Rethinking the intercultural educational approach to folktales. *Children's Literature in Education 50*, 315–332. https://doi.org/10.1007/s10583-017-9330-x

Dervin, F. (2016). *Interculturality in education: A theoretical and methodological toolbox*. Palgrave Macmillan. https://doi.org/10.1057/978-1-137-54544-2

Dervin, F. (2020). Creating and combining models of intercultural competence for teacher education/training: On the need to rethink IC frequently. In F. Dervin, R. Moloney, & A. Simpson (Eds.), *Intercultural competence in the work of teachers: Confronting ideologies and practices* (pp. 57–72). Routledge.

Dervin, F. (2022). *Interculturality in fragments: A reflexive approach*. London: Springer

Dervin, F., & R'boul, H. (2022). *Through the looking-glass of interculturality: Autocritiques*. Springer.

Dervin, F., & Tan, H. (2022). *Supercriticality and interculturality*. Springer.

Dostoyevsky, F. (2014) *The gospel in Dostoyevsky. Selections from his works*. Plough Publishing House.

Esteves, K. J. (2018). Fostering global perspectives with children's literature. *Kappa Delta Pi Record, 54*(2), 72–77. https://doi.org/10.1080/00228958.2018.1443673

Glamour. (2018). 70 women ages 5–75: What does it mean to be in love? www.youtube.com/watch?v=U2oD2sZlQlw

Glamour. (2019). 70 women ages 5–75: What do you find offensive? www.youtube.com/watch?v=dOaFauNcJ2U

Hamer, N. (2019). The hybrid exhibits of the story museum: The child as creative artist and the limits to hands-on participation. *Museum & Society, 17*(3), 390–403. https://doi.org/10.29311/mas.v17i3.3256

Hosseini, K. (2010). *The complete Khaled Hosseini*. Bloomsbury.

Iwai, Y. (2015). Using multicultural children's literature to teach diverse perspectives. *Kappa Delta Pi Record*, *51*(2), 81–86. https://doi.org/10.1080/00228958.2015.1023142

Magos, K., Tsilimeni, T., & Spanopoulou, K. (2013). 'Good morning Alex – Kalimera Maria': Digital communities and intercultural dimension in early childhood education. *Intercultural Education*, *24*(4), 366–373. https://doi.org/10.1080/14675986.2013.812401

Melin, V., & Wagner, B. (2015). The intercultural and non-formal learning processes of children in primary school exchange programmes in France and Germany. *Research in Comparative & International Education*, *10*(3), 407–422. https://doi.org/10.1177/1745499915581079

Młynarczuk-Sokołowska, A. (2022). Intercultural non-formal education: What the children think. *Intercultural Education*, *33*(1), 82–98. https://doi.org/10.1080/14675986.2021.2018171

Newstreet, C., Sarker, A., & Shearer, R. (2018). Teaching empathy: Exploring multiple perspectives to address islamophobia through children's literature. *The Reading Teacher*, *72*(5), 559–568. https://doi.org/10.1002/trtr.1764

Piipponen, O., & Karlsson, L. (2021). *'Our stories were pretty weird too'* – Children as creators of a shared narrative culture in an intercultural story and drawing exchange. *International Journal of Educational Research*, *106*, 1–12. https://doi.org/10.1016/j.ijer.2020.101720

de Saint-Exupery, A. (2015). *The little prince*. Picador Classic.

Scoffham, S. (2019). The world in their heads: Children's ideas about other nations, peoples and cultures. *International Research in Geographical and Environmental Education*, *28*(2), 89–102. https://doi.org/10.1080/10382046.2019.1529712

Tomé-Fernández, M., Senís-Fernández, J., & Ruiz-Martín, D. (2019). Values and intercultural experiences through picture books. *The Reading Teacher*, *73*(2), 205–213. https://doi.org/10.1002/trtr.1813

Torres, H. J. (2019). "They have their own way, and you should respect that": Investigating the outcomes of an elementary world cultures curriculum. *Theory & Research in Social Education*, *47*(4), 548–576. https://doi.org/10.1080/00933104.2019.1653803

Tournebise, C. (2012). *Enseigner l'interculturel dans le supérieur: quels discours et approches d'un concept ambigu à l'heure de l'internationalisation? Le cas de la Finlande*. Humanoria.

Walton, J., Priest, N., & Paradies, Y. (2013). Identifying and developing effective approaches to foster intercultural understanding in schools. *Intercultural Education*, *24*(3), 181–194. https://doi.org/10.1080/14675986.2013.793036

Welply, O. (2018). 'I'm not being offensive but . . .': intersecting discourses of discrimination towards Muslim children in school. *Race Ethnicity and Education*, *21*(3), 370–389. https://doi.org/10.1080/13613324.2017.1294569

Yuan, M., Sude, Wang, T., Zhang, W., Chen, N., Simpson, A., & Dervin, F. (2020). Chinese Minzu education in higher education: An inspiration for 'western' diversity education? *British Journal of Educational Studies*, *68*(4), 461–486. https://doi.org/10.1080/00071005.2020.1712323

2 Interculturality and children

A global film and media perspective

Andreas Jacobsson

Introduction

In this chapter I start with engaging in a theoretical discussion of the notion of interculturality and follow up by discussing and analyzing how to introduce children to interculturality with the support of audio-visual media, in the form of film, television and to some extent, digital and social media. For this discussion to be as clear and helpful as possible, and to be updated with current ideas with relevance for the topic of children and interculturality, I will take a few detours and revisit basic and foundational ideas and concepts from the field of interculturality to clarify my conceptual and methodological positioning before I move forward. So, if you bear with me for a few pages, I will gradually move toward the topic of interest in this book – children and interculturality.

As has already been stated in the introduction, to introduce interculturality to children is underrepresented as a perspective in the field of interculturality – as is focusing on audio-visual representations. Studies on interculturality as a matter for, with and about children is not as frequent as other topics in the different fields where the notion of interculturality is the main focal point for research and education. However, by scrutinizing the previous research in other fields of study it becomes evident that there is already a growing interest in interculturality in, for example, the field of education and in Early Childhood Education and Care (ECEC), mainly focusing on interculturality *about* children from the perspective of teachers and educators (e.g., Björk-Willén et al., 2013; Jacobsson, 2022; Layne & Dervin, 2016).

Predominantly the notion of interculturality in education has been addressed from the perspective of teaching and learning in multicultural and multilingual classrooms (Lash et al., 2022; Walton et al., 2013). A strand of research has focused on teachers' engagement with interculturality (Hajisoteriou & Angelides, 2015; Roiha & Sommier, 2021; Vázquez-Zentella et al., 2017). There are also a growing number of studies focusing on how

DOI: 10.4324/9781003279341-3

to introduce children to interculturality in educational settings with the support of storytelling, children's literature, dramatizations and reading aloud (Oberhuemer, 1994; Piipponen, 2022; Short & Thomas, 2011; see review in chapter 1). In many cases this entails connecting interculturality with literacy and multilingualism from the perspective of teaching interculturality *to* children (Gilmore et al., 2020).

A related scholarly focus worth taking into consideration includes studies that focus on human rights, and specifically the UN Convention of the Rights of the Child (UNCRC) (United Nations, 1998), which has garnered substantial attention in educational sciences during the last decade (e.g., Karlsson Häikiö et al., 2020). The attention has turned into vibrant and sometimes 'dissensual' discourses on access to education in different parts of the world, opening for a deeper understanding of differences between educational contexts (e.g., Wells, 2021). Another issue with relevance for the topic of interculturality and children, that has followed in the footsteps of the global ratification of the UNCRC, is the discourses highlighting children's potential agency and individualism, even at a very early age (Baraldi, 2021; Hammersley, 2017; Prout, 2000). Of particular interest is the debate that has followed about the extent to which the UNCRC is valid globally for all children regardless of cultural contexts, or rather if it is a document promoting and imposing Western liberal ideas of individualism, stipulating how a good childhood should be constituted under the guise of 'universality' (e.g., Baraldi, 2021).

A group of scholars have expanded the focus on so-called multicultural classrooms to include interculturality as relations between educational contexts and children's leisure time and/or home environments (Conde-Pompido et al., 2018; Kwon, 2021). If I enlarge my search for previous research outside of the narrow frame of interculturality there is also a growing number of scholars investigating other topics in education that can be considered close to and relevant for interculturality and children – for example, *social justice and democracy* as well as *inequity and inequality* (Hellman & Lauritsen, 2017; Kessler & Swadener, 2020). Discussions of global and comparative perspectives on childhood/s have also gained substantial attention in other academic fields of study. In the field of *childhood studies* we find research in the cross-section between anthropology, cultural studies, developmental psychology, education, history and sociology (Hsiung, 2005; Imoh et al., 2019; Kregan & Cuthbert, 2014; Lancy, 2022; Montgomery, 2009; Rogoff, 2003; Sommer, 2005; Wells, 2020). These studies have a lot to offer regarding children and interculturality both theoretically and empirically – even if they rarely or ever mention the term interculturality.

In describing these already existing and closely related takes on children and interculturality an apparent question that is relatively, in most cases, unanswered concerns how researchers conceptualize interculturality: What kind of interculturality are they applying in their studies? The general impression is that interculturality is treated as a taken for granted and transparent concept, that is only rarely problematized, or for that matter, perceived as necessary to discuss and open up. A potential reason for this lack of critical scrutiny is that the concept of *culture* in general is perceived as equivalent with national cultural belonging and this understanding is often transferred to interculturality, with the assumption that according to common sense interculturality equals comparisons between national cultures. From my reading of the previous literature that specifically targets children and interculturality it seems that this interpretation is even more dominant than in studies on adults and interculturality (e.g., Młynarczuk-Sokołowska, 2022). However, a distinction must be made between scholars who are based in other academic subjects and are using interculturality as simply an add-on in their studies, and scholars who are, so to speak, already part of the research field and are using interculturality as one of their main theoretical concepts. The latter group are often familiar with the recent critically inclined scholarship that have problematized too simplistic uses of culture and interculturality (e.g., Aman, 2014, 2018; Dervin, 2011, 2016; Ferri, 2018; Holliday, 2010; Piller, 2010; R'Boul, 2022). Regardless of this awareness the pattern of simplistic national cultural comparisons appears to be often repeated. This is very problematic and in the long run it might undermine the validity of the concept in research (Dervin & Jacobsson, 2022).

In what follows, I will introduce my understanding of the multifaceted and polysemic notion of interculturality. I will also expand on how critical interculturality can be discussed as a topic of general relevance in contemporary societies from global perspectives to prepare for approaching children and interculturality. As I see it, it is vital that interculturality in relation to children is part of the ongoing critical rethinking of the field of interculturality. Thereafter I will expand on the conceptualization of childhood/s and discuss different ideas on 'global childhoods'. In the final section of the chapter the focus is on what (critical) interculturality can be potentially developed in relation to, for and about children by focusing on empirical examples of audio-visual film and media representations.

A cross-disciplinary, problematic notion with many faces

Interculturality has for a long time been used (as well as abused) for different reasons in multiple ways in different academic contexts and discourses, and to top that off also in media and political discourses (e.g., Dervin, 2015;

Dervin & Jacobsson, 2022). It is therefore necessary that I start by establishing a tentative definition of the notion to create a common ground for forthcoming dialogues and critical discussions about the notion in relation to children. The ambition with this book is to provide a fertile ground for dialogue with researchers, educators and students with an interest in interculturality in general and with interculturality and children more specifically. It is not in my interest to impose our own definition as the final 'true' and correct interpretation for everyone to use universally. However, in order to avoid miscommunication and outright confusion, which is all too common in discourses regarding interculturality, and to be able to productively use the notion in relation to children it is essential that I clarify our theoretical position. My initial theoretical standpoint is that I have chosen to use the term interculturality and not any other similar term, as *crosscultural, multicultural, trans-cultural* or *polycultural*. These competing and/or complementary terms are often used for similar and/or overlapping reasons, and it can be quite hard to properly distinguish the meaning(s) they contain and why scholars or educators prefer one concept to another.

With that said it is not completely arbitrary which term is used as (to a certain extent) they signal connections to traditions of scholarship, strands of thinking and geopolitical contexts. The reason I use interculturality has to do with both these aspects: 1) my research is and has for a long time been connected to interculturality and intercultural communication education, and my work has been developed in dialogue with studies and scholars in the field; 2) the fact that the prefix *inter-* means 'in between' is in line with how I epistemologically and philosophically approach the field. I are primarily interested in what is taking place 'in between'; I ascertain that something qualitatively new is produced when people meet and interact. Individual experiences and cultural and linguistic backgrounds are always a part of us that we bring with us. However, the kind(s) of meaning(s) that is/are attached to our presence and that we are producing together with other people is/are – as I see it – an open question. This approach to interculturality – as taking place in specific contexts producing meaning – differs from how many other scholars in the field theorize interculturality. It is particularly important to distinguish this approach from the strand of intercultural research that still is theoretically informed by a deterministic understanding of culture, assuming that culture is a trait people carries with them, influencing their behavior and is possible to both generalize and anticipate.

The way I activate interculturality in this chapter is as a notion that captures *processes of cultural encounters* that are simultaneously taking place on different and intersecting socio-political levels in societies – within and across actual and/or perceived borders/boundaries. These processes of diversity are to a certain extent connected to different 'glocal' contexts, intersecting both local and global contexts at the same time (Robertson, 1992). The *movement* of people – for many different reasons – is the sign of the times and constitutes contemporary (globalized) societies (Nail, 2015). However, for understanding interculturality we cannot be content with people who are moving about and meeting other people as our unit of analysis, we also have to take the movement of ideas, representations, goods and money, as well as mediations and representations in the form of film, literature, television, social media etc., into consideration to grasp the complexity of interculturality. My contention is that all contexts are, to a certain extent, glocal in the sense that some kind of cultural encounters are always taking place and that it has had an influence in any given society. Depending on the geopolitical and ideological structures the meaning of all these cultural encounters can be more or less intense, but they are always in the here and now and constantly shifting. I am here proposing that what is important for anyone who wishes to understand interculturality is to practice how to analyze these complex processes in relation to the context(s) which are in focus.

By extending the notion of interculturality to include aspects other than people meeting and interacting with each other, is to stress the fact that analyzing interculturality is to take different levels of experience into consideration simultaneously. It is of course possible and valid to pinpoint a singular aspect for analysis – for example focusing solely on individuals meeting in a specific context at a certain time – as long as the scholar who is performing the analysis is aware of the fact that interculturality is always multi-layered and complex. In research about and with children complexity is often reduced to sensitive and multifaceted issues. Simplified approaches may, for different reasons, appear necessary in relation to children. However, it is necessary to motivate and problematize how and why an approach is adapted specifically to children.

An example of a particularly tricky question that is rarely problematized in research is *when does interculturality start and end?* (Dervin, 2016). This question becomes particularly complex if one agrees with the idea that interculturality consists of constantly ongoing processes. Is it possible to decide when interculturality becomes relevant to investigate and when it ends? Is this even relevant to consider these issues? On an overarching level interculturality is always present in globalized and multicultural societies. However, in relation to introducing children to interculturality, it is a highly relevant question to reflect on further. From my perspective, to pose the question of when interculturality starts motivates scholars to clarify why they think that children should be introduced to interculturality and in what context(s) – home, leisure time, educational settings, in mediated forms, or as a combination of different contexts. The question of when it ends coincides with when children stop being children and are regarded as adults.

Another aspect that is important in relation to the introduction of interculturality to children is to investigate what is keeping groups of people together and creating a sense of belonging – the so-called 'social glue' that is often mentioned by anthropologists and sociologists. This figure of thought is regularly present in studies of children and interculturality, often pushing for the importance for children to develop their identity while growing up. In the Swedish national curricula for preschool (LPFÖ18) for example, it is formulated as vital for young children to be able to develop *their* cultural identity and *their* language. In the way that these ideas are formulated in the curriculum the risk is that children will be categorized as the Other, although with good intentions. This process of othering children is also known as 'culturalization', that is to say categorizing children according to a perceived group identity in relation to ethnicity or nationality, or sometimes as 'racialization' since it is often based on visible difference rather than anything else. It is no surprise that these discourses are present in national curricula since education is a particularly strong arena for developing national belonging – the education of children is, so to speak, to a high extent permeated with national sentiments.

Educational studies on children and interculturality regularly contribute to an 'us and them' categorization. Turning to intercultural studies the fact that this field is also infused with a strong inclination for othering can be explained by the close affinity with anthropology, not the least when interculturality was developed as an academic notion (e.g., Hall, 1959). However, in comparison with intercultural communication education, anthropology was critically rethought during the 1970s and 1980s. Anthropology's characteristics of Western thinking, othering and colonial heritage were pinpointed and criticized (Fabian, 2014). Intercultural communication education did not follow suit until the early 2000s, which, unfortunately, has resulted in a repetitive pattern of othering. In the best of worlds, simplistic solutions to complex issues would be a thing of the past. However, recently a 'turn' to relying on hard sciences such as cognition studies, psychology and brain research as explanations for cultural and social issues has started to become popular. From my perspective this is a step back to fixed categories and othering, only with a different terminology (e.g., Green, 2014).

The alluring simplicity of intercultural competence

The main source for understanding the stronghold othering has had and still has over intercultural communication education is to be found in the most vocal proponents for the idea of turning knowledge about (fixed) national cultural differences into practice in the form of *intercultural competence*. Intercultural competence was at the center of the influential organizational psychologist Gert Hofstede's (2001) surveys and publications in intercultural communication education – promoting the idea of 'cultural dimensions' as a specific tool for understanding individual's social interaction, thinking and behavior according to national cultural patterns. The aim of his model was to develop intercultural competence for understanding, adapting to and communicating with people according to their national cultural background.

Hofstede (2001) developed a theoretical framework for measuring national cultural differences consisting of so-called 'cultural dimensions', capturing perceived core values in different countries. The most well-known dimension is called 'individualism-collectivism' which has been influential beyond intercultural communication education. Dividing the world into individualist and collectivist (national) cultures follows a logic that is presenting a demarcation line between the West and the rest – (or the Global North and Global South with an updated terminology). A clear pattern that is possible to discern in Hofstede's dimensions is that Western liberal ideas of individualism, independence and self-fulfillment are evaluated as positive and modern values, whereas collectivism is regarded as traditional or ideological in a backward sense (Fougère & Moulette, 2007). The use of these dimensions for explaining differences in societal structures according to cultural values is to disregard the existence of different ideologies, the globalization of world economy and the effects of the long history of colonialism and imperialism that have produced unequal opportunities from a global perspective. Reducing the framework for explaining cultural differences such as financial inequity, poverty and social safety nets as attached to family structures instead of being, for example, state-run to cultural differences is to place a very strong emphasis on determinist factors in people's lives.

A cultural value model with striking similarities to Hofstede is the World Values Survey (WVS) that is regularly updating its surveys presenting value-maps where the countries of the world are placed on two axes according to the measuring of core values in nation states. The pattern of attaching a positive note to Western liberal-democratic values is repeated and enhanced by dividing the world into so-called traditional and modern societies according to values. From my point of view, it is vital to refrain from using these studies as a basis for discussing intercultural competence.

The perception of national cultural differences has also made up the foundation for the development of different models of *intercultural competence* promoted in educational research (e.g., Byram, 1997) as well as by supranational organizations such as the Council of Europe (Huber & Reynolds, 2014) and the UNESCO (Deardorff, 2020). For supranational organizations whose primary mission it is to promote *international relations*, it is just common sense to regard interculturality as an aspect of international relations adjusted for learning how to get along despite cultural and communicative differences. Since these organizations have been very influential for the implementation of interculturality in educational systems, from both a European and a global perspective, their national cultural interpretation of interculturality has become normalized in education, in political discourses and in media discourses. The ideas that are promoted by the supranational organizations – to develop competences for living together harmoniously in diversity – are communicated as ideologically neutral responses to specific social problems. Interestingly, in a recent document published by the Council of Europe (2016), intercultural competence was replaced by 'democratic' competence, clearly showing that it is Western and European liberal values that make up the ideology of the concept of intercultural competence at least in the European context (Dervin, 2017).

In previous publications together with Fred, we have criticized the idea of developing intercultural competence as a culturalist, reductionistic and Eurocentric endeavor (Dervin & Jacobsson, 2021a, 2021b). The main problem regarding intercultural competence is threefold: 1) it reduces individuals to representatives of specific national groups of people and upholds what can be described as a unidirectional ethnographic viewpoint – forcing the interculturally competent individual to be looking at and evaluating the non-European Other and thereby establishing a categorization of 'us vs. them'; 2) it is communicated as a deceptively simple, efficient and functionalist tool set for dealing with complex social problems by influential supranational organizations; 3) it oscillates between framing Western/European values on the one hand as ideologically neutral, and on the other hand as universally positive values (democratic, liberal, individualist), that in the best of worlds, should be globally accepted.

It is from my perspective not enough to refine and produce a 'better' version of intercultural competence. I am proposing instead that as a necessary step to rethink interculturality, it is necessary to completely disregard the term intercultural competence. To reproduce the ideas of intercultural competence on these premises to children in any settings, be it in their homes, in educational settings or in research, should be avoided. We simply cannot introduce children to ideas about interculturality that are so clearly simplified with a good conscience.

Critical perspectives and interculturalizing interculturality

As I have already touched upon earlier in this chapter, a strand of scholars have pinpointed and criticized an array of strikingly problematic issues in the field, and thereby initiated a response to the traditionally dominant ideas of interculturality – intercultural competence; the reductionist comparisons between national cultural frameworks as determining patterns of behavior; and finally, the Eurocentric perspective/s permeating the foundational ideas. Criticality is nowadays a familiar aspect of research on interculturality.

Predominantly the focus of critical interculturality has been to problematize the use of *culture*. In general culture has been framed as an anthropological concept in intercultural studies and understood as capturing collective identities and explaining all kinds of thinking and behavior according to group belonging (e.g., Breidenbach & Nyíri, 2009; Dervin, 2015). As I have previously concluded this focus has consolidated an outdated 'anthropological' understanding of culture in the form of an essentialist and deterministic notion describing *Otherness* as fixed over time, from generation to generation (Fabian, 2014). Critical scholars in education have developed this further by highlighting the inherent Eurocentrism in the field (Aman, 2015; Dervin, 2011, 2015, 2016; Dervin & Jacobsson, 2022; R'Boul, 2022). A critical term that has gained in popularity for clarifying the Western-centric bias and the regularly condescending treatment of alternative ways of thinking outside of the Western social science paradigm is *decolonial* (Aman, 2014, 2018; Gorski, 2008). More and more critical voices are advocating for the importance of *decolonizing* everything from teaching and research to curricula and textbooks, to come to terms with Eurocentric structures and a colonial heritage in the production of knowledge. However, in many cases, 'decolonial' seems to fill the function of a catchphrase rather than a properly critical concept. An exception is the thought-provoking and radical interpretation of 'decolonizing interculturality' introduced by Robert Aman (2018) as *inter-epistemology*. Aman illustrates how consistently Eurocentric the theorization in intercultural education still is and proposes several solutions such as epistemological meetings and exchanges of knowledge and philosophical ideas from different parts of the world.

To take on Aman's challenging ideas, scholars of interculturality must widen their scope of interest, taking part in scholarship in languages other than English and relativize their epistemological foundation. An important step toward achieving inter-epistemology is to problematize a taken-for-granted positivist scientism that has permeated all interculturality connected to the functionalist interpretations of intercultural competence (Dervin & Jacobsson, 2022; Holliday & MacDonald, 2021). In different academic contexts and in different languages around the world there are different interpretations of interculturality (Dervin & Yuan, 2021). And since interculturality is a wide-spread cross-disciplinary concept, scholars who are working in the same context can also have very different ways of understanding and applying the notion, which makes the situation even more complex.

Together, Fred and I have recently introduced an approach that we have labelled *interculturalizing interculturality*, where we are striving to achieve a radical movement toward a more inclusive interculturality for scholars and students from a global perspective (see Dervin, 2021; Dervin & Jacobsson, 2021b, 2022). In addition to embracing different epistemologies and knowledge traditions interculturalizing interculturality requires an explicit awareness of different ideologies, global capitalism and a historical knowledge of colonialism and imperialism, in addition to the values that are traditionally at the center of interculturality (Dervin & Jacobsson, 2022). The reason that motivates our current rethinking of interculturality in this way is that we are dissatisfied with the current Western epistemological dominance. Regardless of if you are a researcher and/or teacher, in most educational contexts in the world Western conceptualizations of interculturality are given precedence. If we are even thinking of treating the prefix *inter-* of interculturality in a serious manner and regard ourselves as intercultural scholars, we are obliged to act against this epistemological inequality.

This a demanding task that requires strenuous efforts from individual researchers. To come to terms with these issues that are methodological, theoretical as well as ideological always has to be a collective endeavor, that is developed in dialogue with a cross-disciplinary and multilingual global research community. Turning our attention to introducing interculturality to children, to strive for interculturalizing interculturality becomes even more pertinent. From that perspective my effort in this chapter is a piece of a larger puzzle, although, since it regards children, a very important one.

Global Childhood/s and interculturalizing interculturality for children

Turning my attention to a strategic selection of studies from the recently developed cross-disciplinary field of childhood studies that has gathered scholars from anthropology, cultural, studies, education, media studies and sociology several important ideas appear that can be treated as insightful lessons for intercultural scholars with an interest in children. There is a general agreement in childhood studies that children's lives are turning out differently depending on where they live and are brought up – their lives are so to speak 'shaped by social and cultural expectations adults and their peers have of them in different times and places' (Wells, 2020, p. 3). This entails that the concept of childhood shifts between different geopolitical contexts, over time (e.g., Montgomery, 2009; Wells, 2020).

How children are perceived and understood from different perspectives is connected to what can be described as specific *visions of childhood* that are circulating in different societies. These visions – or sometimes even better described as *idealizations* – can be found among adults, in scholarship, the media, education and political discourses (among others). Not individually but together as a field of studies, highlighting the presence of the visions of childhood in different societies, and thereafter contrasting them with studies on children's actual living conditions, scholars in childhood studies perform what, according to me, can be considered as an unspoken initiative for *interculturalizing interculturality*. Childhood studies represents as such an initiative where complexity is taken into consideration. However, I am not suggesting that individual scholars are responsible for singlehandedly do what intercultural scholars are incapable of. My point is that cross-disciplinarity can provide a more wide-scoped understanding of interculturality as processes of diversity – an understanding that appears to be lacking in the field of intercultural communication education, intercultural studies and intercultural education. There is also an underlaying productive tension between social constructivism in sociology and anthropology and the natural sciences in developmental psychology creating an array of dissensual but productive contradictions. Children are, for example, on the one hand, portrayed as biological entities undergoing developmental stages, and, on the other hand, as representatives of cultural formations (e.g., Sommer, 2005). The inherent contradictions are contributing to a complexity of childhood studies.

For many scholars with a specific interest in children and childhoods, studying children is not only a research interest, but also a politically and ideologically informed decision to take a stand for and support children. For example, by producing knowledge that strengthens children's position as being part of a 'subordinate' group in society; by promoting children's rights in the society or globally; by highlighting a specific child-related issue as, for example, abuse and violence, bullying, homelessness, poverty, identity, gender and/or sexuality. Hammersley (2017) argues that the formation of childhood studies as an academic subject is possible to compare with other recently developed fields of study such as feminist studies, gender studies and critical race studies. This politically motivated research inclination clarifies the importance to activate an awareness of the researcher's perspective in studies where children are the object of analysis. This is also in line with the idea of interculturalizing interculturality in the sense that culture is just one aspect among many others to include in the analysis of interculturality. Ideologies, politics and historical circumstances as well as researchers' own positions are equally important (and maybe more so) to include in an 'intercultural' analysis. But what is lacking in childhood studies is precisely a critically developed understanding of culture, which, I argue, critical interculturality could provide.

It is not just the empirical studies and the global approach in childhood studies that intercultural scholars can be inspired by. I am proposing that to be able to introduce children to interculturality as a scholar and/or an educator we have to familiarize ourselves with the cross-section between intercultural communication education and childhood studies.

Media cultures, children's perspectives and 'childism'

Introducing interculturality to children is a very complex thing to do. Not the least since children are an exceptionally heterogenous group to target. One way of approaching this daunting task is to make use of media representations. As already stated in the introduction to this chapter and in the previous chapter, for a long time, literature has been the preferred medium for introducing interculturality to children in educational settings from a global perspective (e.g., Piipponen, 2022). There are several reasons for this situation. The first reason is that literature and reading aloud for children are regarded as directly beneficial for children's language development and are therefore often used as popular tools by teachers as well as by parents and other caretakers. The second and equally important reason is that literature is in many contexts a highly regarded 'art form'. Even though children's literature is seldom treated as 'proper' high art, it has a much better reputation than other forms of media.

I have previously maintained that there is a lot to gain from using world cinema and other global audio-visual media as the primary source for introducing interculturality – and for developing a deeper understanding in the form of thinking with film about interculturality (Dervin & Jacobsson, 2022; Jacobsson, 2017). The concept of world cinema is an umbrella term that captures film cultures that are outside of the location where the viewer is situated. This means that what is considered as world cinema shifts with the viewer's geopolitical position, and what is center and what is periphery are relativized. In this interpretation world cinema is a radical tool for thinking about the world in terms of equality.

World cinema is today highly accessible and affordable in most geographical contexts. The advantages of using world cinema are that the audio-visual experiences, on the one hand, provide an insight into different environments, and on the other hand, that viewing world cinema may be regarded as an intercultural encounter in its own right. Audio-visual representations are simultaneously activating cognition and emotion in a more direct manner than literature. This makes film particularly interesting to use for introducing children to interculturality (Grodal, 2009; Jacobsson, 2017). However, film and other audio-visual media, digital media and social media are rarely regarded as media with great potential for children's learning. Instead, these media are considered with suspicion and as threats to children's wellbeing. Swedish film and media scholar Margareta Rönnberg (2003) pinpoints that the bad reputation that audio-visual media often are ascribed in relation to children is rooted in adult idealistic visions of childhood and a long tradition of regarding children as 'innocent' and in need of protection. For Rönnberg (2003) this is a clear expression of an overarching adult-centered approach that can be described as an intergenerational hierarchical and patronizing understanding of children. Another reason for the preference for literature is that scholars, teachers and parents believe that reading is perceived as an active process whereas film viewing a passive activity. The myth of the passive spectator has been particularly strong and long-lived in discussion of children and media consumption. Despite being repeatedly proven false this myth regularly attracts new generations of adults (e.g., Buckingham, 2007).

Turning to Rönnberg (2003) for support, this would be an example of how adults interpret children's media consumption from an adult perspective, failing to change perspectives and understand children's points of view. To come to terms with the always present generational inequality, Rönnberg (2003) promotes a radical interpretation of the concept of 'childism' (in Swedish 'barnism'), comparable with feminism in the sense that it requires supporting all children based on their own perspectives. According to Rönnberg many researchers state that they are applying a children's perspective in their studies but are not fulfilling their claim. They mostly apply a 'child perspective' in their studies which is to study children from an outside position, rather than applying a children's perspective where children's perceptions, voices, thoughts and ideas are considered in their own right (Sommer et al., 2010; see chapter 1).

For Rönnberg (2003) children are the only producers of children's culture. Culture produced for children by grown-ups can never be 'children's culture' unless it is altered by children and used in, for example, children's play activities. Rönnberg's most radical and provocative childist statement is that adults are regularly destroying children's play activities by interfering and trying to 'help' them. The harshest critique is directed toward teachers who, according to Rönnberg, fail to accept that playing and learning as a child are free, liberating and anarchic endeavors (Rönnberg, 2003). From this perspective adults' perceptions of normativity are suppressing children's potential by regulating their culture and play. In the words of the influential play scholar Brian Sutton-Smith:

> It seems that the history of the imagination in childhood is a history of an ever greater suppression and rationalization of the irrational.

> Paradoxically children, who are supposed to be the players among us, are allowed much less freedom for irrational, wild, dark, or deep play in Western culture than are adults who are thought no to play at all
>
> (Sutton-Smith, 1997, p. 151).

This discussion on childism, children's culture and play, is of course connected to a Nordic and Western cultural perspective on children. However, this discussion opens several important methodological aspects to include in a framework for considering interculturality and children:

- An important aspect of interculturality is to be able to shift perspectives. The 'childist' standpoint clarifies that to introduce interculturality to children requires that we also include children's perspectives to help us think carefully about what this entails,
- It adds another layer to the complexity of the concept of culture by stating that children's culture is qualitatively different from other forms of culture and children *should* be allowed to have agency in their own play activities,
- It introduces the concept of 'intergenerational' as an additional important aspect of interculturality,
- It clarifies that audio-visual media are highly important for contemporary 'children's culture' and are not making children passive in their interaction with media representations.

This line of thinking is radically child-oriented and promotes intergenerational equality. From an intercultural perspective this must be problematized. As the field of childhood studies has clarified, children's lives look very different in different parts of the world, and 'children's cultures' can never be a homogenous concept. This is vital to keep in mind while striving for understanding children's perspectives. If we agree that play is children's way of processing experiences in their everyday life, *how* children play also differs in different cultural contexts. This is also vital to keep in mind while introducing interculturality to children. Finally, it is also important to acknowledge that the notion of play as a liberating space for children is an idealization that requires that all children have equal access to the play arena, which of course, is not necessarily the case. Children may be excluded from playing with other children for many different reasons. Some children are never included or invited to play and, from an adult perspective, not to interfere in children's activities when children are bullied or excluded for other reasons would be both hard and problematic.

Audio-visual examples for introducing children to interculturality

To use world cinema is an important and efficient way to introduce children to interculturality and give an insight into the different 'worlds' that children inhabit. I have previously argued that world cinema can be used as a tool for opening for different viewer positions and perspectives for adult spectators (Jacobsson, 2017). Here I extend this argument to include children. It is equally important for children to experience audio-visual depictions from different parts of the world. And since watching films can be regarded as intercultural encounters to be taken as seriously as actual encounters, world cinema can be used to interculturalize interculturality for children. To a certain extent I argue that children can watch world films on their own as part of being introduced to interculturality, however the films that I discuss in the following sections are intended to be watched together with teachers and/ or parents to follow up the experience with discussions with the children. In a similar manner as read aloud activities in kindergartens, preschools and schools are regarded as more efficient for learning and understanding if they are followed by qualitative and planned discussions together with the children. The term *film* is used as a polysemic word in this chapter, capturing a variety of genres, such as fiction films, documentaries, short films and animated films. There are of course differences between these genres that are fruitful to include in discussions with children – not the least in relation to the truth-value of the depictions. However, I make no distinction between genres regarding the efficiency for introducing children to interculturality. If the film captures the children's interest in any way, it is worth using.

To select examples for carrying out analyses of audio-visual representations based on a theoretical framework for introducing interculturality is a particularly risky business. The first problem is that by choosing a film that I consider as world cinema with the potential of offering an intercultural experience for children, I depart from my specific geopolitical position. By doing that I am at the same time depriving everyone else from their relative position and fixate what world cinema and intercultural perspectives can potentially be. With this disclaimer I would like to emphasize that the examples that I have chosen to discuss here are just some of the numerous potential examples available and should in no way be considered as specifically important examples from a global perspective. A way to handle this particular conundrum is to always include a meta-perspective when choosing a film and motivate for oneself on which grounds the specific film is important for introducing interculturality to children.

A strong example of a world film that depicts what Robert Aman discusses as inter-epistemic aspects of interculturality is *Keita – L'héritage du griot*[1] (Burkina Faso, 1995). The film was directed by Dani Kouyate and tells the story of a young boy. One day a griot (a traditional West African storyteller) approaches the boy at his home to tell the story of his name, to introduce the boy by oral narration to his history. The boy becomes mesmerized by the griot's story, and he starts to skip school to be able to stay home and listen to the story. The boy's parents are annoyed with their son and want him to go to school to get a good education and to become someone in life, and only listen to traditional stories at his leisure time. By juxtaposing a 'modern' education with 'traditional' knowledge the film problematizes different epistemologies and clarifies in the end that both traditions can co-exist in an inter-epistemic dialogue. This is a film that would work very well to introduce children concisely to complex issues of why we need to take different epistemologies into consideration, and why there is not one truth or one way to know things. *Keita – L'héritage du griot* is a film that can be characterized as a 'family film' suitable for young children from the age of 6.

Another aspect of interculturalizing interculturality is to focus on how material differences connected to geopolitical and economic inequalities affect children's lives. Staying in the sub-Saharan region of Africa but turning to another film culture, the Malian film *Nyamanton* (Cheick Oumar Sissoko, 1986), includes a striking opening sequence where children to be able to take part in education have to bring their own school benches to class, which they had to build on their own from parts that they found among the garbage. The film tells a story about two poor siblings who spend their days finding things to sell in garbage piles to help their family survive and to afford going to school. There are numerous examples of films that depict the effects of social and economic inequality on children, but *Nyamanton* is a rare example when it comes to carefully integrating children's perspectives in the narration as well as in the camera angles. This film can be used together with children as young as three to four years of age.

A film culture that is filled with films focusing on children's issues and children's perspectives is found in Iran. A classic example is Amir Naderi's *The Runner/Davendeh* (1984) that tells the story of poor young boy. To find a way to move forward in life he enrolls in school but is soon facing conflicts with the other children. To find a solution and impress his classmates he enters a spelling competition. From this perspective the film presents a strong case for children's agency and ability to make their own independent decisions about their life during harsh circumstances. In *Bashu, the little stranger/Bashu, gharibeye koochak* (Bahram Beizaye, 1989) a young boy who has lost his family and his home in the war between Iran and Iraq has fled to a different part of the country where he is unable to understand the spoken dialect. Eventually, he meets a middle-age woman who raises her sons alone since her husband has left home for work. The film depicts intergenerational, interlingual and intercultural differences in the same country. All this complexity is developed in the relationship between a young boy and a woman in an isolated place in the countryside. The simple storyline makes this film particularly interesting for introducing children from the age of 7–12 to understand interculturality as taking place in as well as between different geographical contexts. There are several more examples of children as protagonists in Iranian cinema. An extra layer of complexity is that, to a certain extent, it has been possible to make films with children in focus to bypass censorship in Iranian film culture. To discuss these films also entails reflecting on adult perspectives on using children as symbols and metaphors of societal, ideological and political issues (e.g., Sadr, 2002).

To use world cinema for introducing children to interculturality entails dealing with different political systems and regulations for filmmaking, which makes film viewing an endeavor saturated with ideological aspects. As I see it, these kinds of sensitive issues are important to address even with very young children. And to discuss them as preconditions in relation to a film that they have seen will make the issues more concrete and possible to understand.

Stereotypes for whom?

In my own experience as a teacher of interculturality in film and media and in early childhood education, when my students are asked to write an assignment with an analysis of mediated interculturality, they often turn to animated Disney films. The reasons for doing this are both to discuss how otherness and intercultural encounters are depicted on film, and to criticize stereotypes in the films. It is certainly true that Disney films have been saturated with gender stereotypes as well as ethno-cultural stereotypes for a very long time. To be fair Disney is not the only production company that has been depicting stereotypes, but since they have reached a global popularity among a wide diversity of audiences with stories about cultural encounters, they are particularly interesting for my students to include in their analyses of interculturality. The reason why I mention this here is because of the many interpretations of Disney's films that I have read where they rarely discuss these issues from children's perspectives. When the ambition is to introduce children to interculturality it is important to keep in mind that for an adult what constitutes a gender stereotype, or an ethno-cultural stereotype may be something quite different from how children interpret the same depictions. In intercultural communication education to identify stereotypes either as a hindrance for intercultural communication or as representations in media is a common and popular research topic. My impression is that studies often fail to problematize different possible interpretations. Here I would like to stress that I find it very important not to impose adult preconceived notions on children's experiences of film and media. I am not stating that we should avoid identifying and discussing stereotypes. However, we should make our interpretations more nuanced and open for different perspectives. This is the only way forward for discussions on stereotypes, should they be part of the process of interculturalizing interculturality.

A particularly telling example of different perspectives on a contemporary film by Disney is the debate that took place in Swedish media after the premiere of *Encanto* (Jared Bush, Byron Howard & Charise Castro-Smith, USA, 2021). The story is about a Colombian family named Madrigal. The family's collective magic is keeping the village Encanto together, but something has changed that is starting to create cracks in the foundation of the magical construction that is the home for the family as well as their friends. The critic Nooisha Shams published an article for a major Swedish daily (Aftonbladet, 22-01-25), trying to understand why the Swedish reception of this film was so lukewarm and negative in comparison with the reception in the US. Her conclusion was that the Swedish critics failed to understand that this film was made in the tradition of Latin American magical realism, focusing on interpersonal family relations. From this perspective what could be regarded as stereotypical and culturalist for the Swedish critics, corresponds to a vibrant musical celebration of a culturally specific genre for another audience.

In a previous animated Disney-film *Coco* (Lee Unkrich & Adrian Molina, USA, 2017), we find another example of how Latin American (film) culture is remolded into a children's film aiming to entertain a wide audience. In this film we encounter the importance of celebrating Día de los Muertos (Day of the Dead) in Mexico. A young boy who is striving to become a musician enters the realm of the dead in search of a relative who was a famous singer and guitarist. As accomplished as the relative was in playing his instruments, as careless he was to take care of his family. The most interesting aspect of this film from the perspective of this book is that the relative is based on the exceptionally popular film star Pedro Infante, from the classical era of Mexican film musicals in the 1930s-1950s. With support of this film that has been very popular among young audiences it is possible to develop children's knowledge about film cultural traditions and how films from different parts of the world are connected and influenced by other traditions in what can be described with the term intertextuality.

By digging deeper into the films, beyond the surface, we can problematize different perceptions of stereotypes together with children. And, of course, we should ask the children how they perceive the depictions in the films and take their opinions seriously.

A documentary on Children's encounters over (impossible) borders

The final example that I discuss in this chapter is a film that made a great emotional impact on me when I first watched it – and it has lingered in my memory ever since. The film in question is the documentary *Promises* (USA, 2001), directed by B. Z. Goldberg, Justine Shapiro and Carlos Bolado. The film depicts how the conflict between Israel and Palestine affects children on both sides of the border from the children's perspectives. This film introduces complex issues and can be used with children age 9–12.

The filmmakers followed seven young children ages eight to twelve years old for three years. The children were all encouraged to speak their mind and present their understanding of the conflict. They also introduced their perceptions of the 'other side' and connected their experiences to their own context and living conditions. The film makers worked consciously with depicting children's perspectives (as theorized in this chapter). The contrasting experiences and ideas that the children had about the Other were treated respectfully by the film makers, and the potential 'adult perspective' was not imposed in the filmic depiction. The filmmakers were involved with the children during the process of the filming and kept a constant dialogue with them about their experiences.

The strategy to introduce different perspectives became even more poignant in the final part of the film when the children from Israel and Palestine finally got the chance to meet and spend time together. They were all living geographically close together but in what they themselves expressed as *completely different worlds* – something that they became aware of when they had to pass several checkpoints on their way to the meeting.

All their preconceived notions about the other were put into play during their interactions. The initial tension was finally released when the children started playing a soccer game together with the film crew. In the play activity they were free to use the tools for getting along and interacting that they all already mastered.

When they parted ways, it was an emotionally charged moment when all the children expressed joy over having had the opportunity to meet and sadness over being separated again. In follow-up interviews the children partly regressed again to their preconceived notions about the other. With this structure I realize that this film is ticking all the theoretical boxes that I have set up for a framework for looking into children and interculturality. The children in the film were allowed to apply their own perspectives, they found a common denominator in playing freely together. In addition to this structuring of the depiction the film visualized with all clarity the very specific living conditions that affected the children's lives in a conflict area.

The emotional expressions in the film were strong and gave the impression of genuine emotions.

This film is a unique example of how to problematize children's experiences of and voices about a conflict that they have not chosen themselves to be part of. The complexity of *Promises* and the potential emotional impact of the story make it more suitable for children age 9–12 when it comes both to watching and discussing it in class. This film needs thorough preparations, and the teacher should have introduced the conflict in advance and clarified some of the reasons and the historical context behind the conflict.

Concluding remarks

To fulfil the ambitions to introduce children to interculturality with support of world cinema, as for example a teacher or a parent, requires some basic preparations:

1) Watch the film in advance,
2) Analyze the film and take different potential perspectives into consideration,
3) Include cultural and film historical aspects in your analysis of the film,
4) Prepare questions for discussing with the child/children.

I have intermittently stressed the importance of different perspectives, including children's perspectives, in this chapter. However, as Margareta Rönnberg highlighted in relation to her interpretation of 'childism', it will always be considered as a type of 'unwelcome' intrusion in children's perspectives and children's culture when adults/teachers/parents introduce interculturality to children. This is something that has to be clear for anyone who is working with these issues, but it is also something that must be accepted, to a certain extent.

An arena for children's own culture that has started to be more and more important in children's lives are different social media apps. On apps such as TikTok, children both take part in depictions and produce their own content (e.g.,. Pomerantz & Field, 2021). The videos on many of these apps are in themselves examples of hybridity and intertextuality that are highly interesting from the perspective of interculturality. A very important aspect of children's interactions with this type of social media is that a lot of what is produced contains replications of other content. When children are producing content, they focus on doing like their peers and they often copy what others have already done. From an adult perspective any ideals of authenticity and originality fail to capture children's culture. This type of communication might actually capture the idea of interculturalizing interculturality

Interculturality and children 71

better than film could ever achieve. But to make use of this material for introducing interculturality to children would require that adults impose their perspective on children . . .

Note

1 I have previously discussed this film in relation to the idea of interculturalizing interculturality, the discussion here is based on my previous analysis (Dervin & Jacobsson, 2022: 55–56).

References

Acevedo, M. V. (2019). Young children playing their way into intercultural understanding. *Journal of Early Childhood Literacy*, *19*(3), 375–398. https://doi.org/10.1177/1468798417727134

Aman, R. (2014). *Impossible interculturality: Education and the colonial difference in a multicultural world* (Linköping Studies in Behavioural Science 182) [Dissertation]. Linköping University.

Aman, R. (2015). Why interculturalidad is not interculturality: Colonial remains and paradoxes in translation between indigenous social movements and supranational bodies. *Cultural Studies*, *29*(2), 205–228. https://doi.org/10.1080/09502386.2014.899379

Aman, R. (2018). *Decolonising intercultural education: Colonial differences, the geopolitics of knowledge, and inter-epistemic dialogue*. Routledge.

Baraldi, C. (2020). Roots and problems of universalism: The concept of children's agency. In C. Baraldi & L. Castro (Eds.), *Global childhoods in international perspective: Universality, diversity, and inequalities* (pp. 15–32). Sage.

Beizaye B. (Director). (1989). *Bashu, gharibeye koochak/Bashu – the little stranger* [Film]. Kanunparvaresh fekri.

Björk-Willén, P., Gruber, S., & Puskás, T. (2013). *Nationell förskola med mångkulturellt uppdrag*. Liber.

Breidenbach, J., & Nyíri, P. (2009). *Seeing culture everywhere: From genocide to consumer habits*. University of Washington Press.

Buckingham, D. (2007). Childhood in the age of global media. *Children's Geographies*, *5*(1–2), 43–54. https://doi.org/10.1080/14733280601108155

Bush, J., Howard, B., & Castro Smith, C. (Directors). (2021). *Encanto* [Film]. Walt Disney Animation Studios/Walt Disney Pictures.

Byram, M. (1997). *Teaching and assessing intercultural communicative competence*. Multilingual Matters.

CoE (Council of Europe). (2016). *Competences for democratic culture*. Council of Europe Publishing.

Conde-Pompido, T., Loos, E., van Wilgenburg, W., Versteeg, M., Aléncar, A., Simons, M., Lamoth, C., & Finkenauer, C. (2018). Using an ice-skating exergame to foster intercultural interaction between refuges and Dutch children. *Cogent Education*, *5*(1). https://doi.org/10.1080/2331186X.2018.1538587

Convention on the rights of the child. (1989). Treaty no. 27531. United Nations Treaty Series, 1577, 3–178.

Cregan, K., & Cuthbert, D. (2014). *Global childhoods: Issues and debates.* Sage.

Deardorff, D. K. (2020). *Manual for developing intercultural competences: Story circles.* Routledge.

Dervin, F. (2015). Towards post-intercultural teacher education: Analysing 'extreme' intercultural dialogue to reconstruct interculturality. *European Journal of Teacher Education, 38*(1), 71–86. https://doi.org/10.1080/02619768.2014.902441

Dervin, F. (2016). *Interculturality in education: A theoretical and methodological toolbox.* Palgrave Macmillan. https://doi.org/10.1057/978-1-137-54544-2

Dervin, F. (2017). Critical turns in language and intercultural communication pedagogy: The simple-complex continuum *(Simplexity)* as a new perspective. In M. Dasli & R. Díaz (Eds.), *The critical turn in language and intercultural communication pedagogy: Theory, research and practice* (pp. 58–72). Routledge.

Dervin, F. (2021). *Critical and reflexive languaging in the construction of interculturality as an object of research and practice* (19 April 2021). Digital series of talks on plurilingualism and interculturality, University of Copenhagen.

Dervin, F., & Jacobsson, A. (2021a). *Teacher education for critical and reflexive interculturality.* Palgrave Macmillan. https://doi.org/10.1007/978-3-030-66337-7

Dervin, F., & Jacobsson, A. (2021b). *Interculturaliser l'interculturel.* L'harmattan.

Dervin, F., & Jacobsson, A. (2022). *Intercultural communication education: Broken realities and rebellious dreams.* Springer. https://doi.org/10.1007/978-981-19-1589-5

Dervin, F., & Yuan, M. (2021). *Revitalizing interculturality in education. Chinese Minzu as a companion.* Routledge.

Fabian, J. (2014/1982). *Time and the other: How anthropology makes its other* (2nd ed.). Columbia University Press.

Ferri, G. (2018). *Intercultural communication: Critical approaches and future challenges.* Cham: Palgrave Macmillan. https://doi.org/10.1007/978-3-319-73918-2

Fougère, M., & Moulette, A. (2007). The construction of the modern West and the backward rest: Studying the discourse of Hofstede's *culture's consequences. Journal of Multicultural Discourses, 2*(1), 1–19. https://doi.org/10.2167/md051.0

Gilmore, G., Margrain, V., & Mellgren, E. (2020). Intercultural literacy dialogue: International assessment moderation in early childhood teacher education. *Intercultural Education, 31*(2), 208–227. https://doi.org/10.1080/14675986.2019.1702293

Goldberg, B. Z., Shapiro, J., & Bolado, C. (2001). Promises [Film]. Promises Film Project.

Gorski, P. (2008). Good intentions are not enough: A declonizing intercultural education. *Intercultural Education, 19*(6), 515–525. https://doi.org/10.1080/14675980802568319

Green, J. (2014). *Moral tribes: Emotion, reason, and the gap between us and them.* Atlantic Books.

Grodal, T. (2009). *Embodied visions: Evolution, emotion, culture, and film.* Oxford University Press.

Hajisoteriou, C., & Angelides, P. (2015). Listening to children's voices on intercultural education policy and practice. *International Journal of Qualitative Studies in Education, 28*(1), 112–130. https://doi.org/10.1080/09518398.2013.872813

Hall, E. T. (1959). *The silent language*. Greenwich: Fawcett Publications.

Hammersley, M. (2017). Childhood studies: A sustainable paradigm? *Childhood 24*(1), 113–127. https://doi.org/10.1177/0907568216631399

Hellman, A., & Lauritsen, K. (Eds.). (2017). *Diversity and social justice in early childhood education: Nordic perspectives*. Cambridge Scholars.

Hofstede, G. (2001). *Culture's consequences – second edition: Comparing values, behaviors, institutions and organizations across Nations*. Sage.

Holliday, A. (2010). *Intercultural communication and ideology*. Sage.

Holliday, A., & MacDonald, M. (2020). Researching the intercultural: Intersubjectivity and the problem with postpositivism. *Applied linguistics, 41*(5), 621–639. https://doi.org/10.1093/applin/amz006

Hsiung, P. C. (2005). *A tender voyage: Children and childhood in late imperial China*. Stanford University Press.

Imoh, A., Bourdillon, M., & Meichsner, S. (Eds.). (2019). *Global childhoods beyond the North- South divide*. Palgrave Macmillan.

Jacobsson, A. (2017). Intercultural film: Fiction film as audiovisual documents of interculturality. *Journal of Intercultural Studies, 38*(1), 54–69. https://doi.org/10.1080/07256868.2017.1269061

Jacobsson, A. (2022). Internationalisation and interculturality in a teacher education programme. *World Studies in Education, 23*(1).

Karlsson Häikiö, T., Sundhall, J., & Asplund-Carlsson, M. (2020). *En lag för barn: Kulturvetenskapliga perspektiv på barnrättskonventionen*. Studentlitteratur.

Kessler, S. A., & Swadener, B. B. (Eds.). (2020). *Educating for social justice in early childhood*. Routledge.

Kouyaté, D. (Director). (1995). *Keita – L'heritage du griot* [Film]. Afix productions/ Les productions de la lanterne/Sahélis productions.

Kwon, J. (2021). Intercultural learning in the home environment: Children's experiences as part of a homestay host family. *Globalisation, Societies and Education, 19*(3), 274–286. https://doi.org/10.1080/14767724.2020.1816923

Lancy. D. F. (2022). *The anthropology of childhood: Cherubs, chattel, changelings* (3rd ed.). Cambridge University press.

Lash, M., Akpovo, S. M., Cushner, K. (2022). Developing the intercultural competence of early childhood preservice teachers: Preparing for culturally diverse classrooms. *Journal of Early Childhood Teacher Education, 43*(1), 105–126. https://doi.org/10.1080/10901027.2020.1832631

Layne, H., & Dervin, F. (2016). Problematizing Finland's pursuit of intercultural (kindergarten) teacher education. *Multicultural Education Review, 8*(2), 118–134. https://doi.org/10.1080/2005615X.2016.1161290

Läroplan för förskolan LPFÖ18. (2018). Stockholm: Skolverket.

Młynarczuk-Sokołowska, A. (2022). Intercultural non-formal education: what the children think. *Intercultural Education, 33*(1), 82–98. https://doi.org/10.1080/14675986.2021.2018171

Montgomery, H. (2009). *An introduction to childhood: Anthropological perspectives on children's lives*. Wiley-Blackwell.
Naderi, A. (Director). (1984). *Davandeh/The runner* [Film]. Kanun pavaresh fekri/ Studio of the voice and portrait of the Islamic revolution of Iran.
Nail, T. (2015). *The figure of the migrant*. Stanford University Press.
Oberhuemer, P. (1994). Stories make a difference: Intercultural dialogue in the early years. *European Early Childhood Education Research Journal*, *2*(1), 35–42. https://doi.org/10.1080/13502939485207511
Piller, I. (2010/2017). *Intercultural communication: A critical introduction*. Edinburgh University Press.
Piipponen, O. (2022). *Children encountering each other through stories: Developing a dynamic approach to interculturality in primary schools* (Dissertations in Education, Humanities, and Theology 179) [Dissertation]. The University of Eastern Finland.
Prout, A. (2000). Childhood bodies: Construction, agency and hybridity. In A. Prout (Ed.), *The body, childhood and society* (pp. 1–18). Macmillan.
R'Boul, H. (2022). Researching the intercultural: Solid/liquid interculturality in Moroccan- themed scholarship. *The Journal of North African Studies*, *27*(3), 441–462. https://doi.org/10.1080/13629387.2020.1814750
Robertson, R. (1992). *Globalization: Social theory and global culture*. Sage.
Rogoff, B. (2003). *The cultural nature of human development*. Oxford University Press.
Roiha. A., & Sommier, M. (2021). Exploring teachers' perceptions and practices of intercultural education in an international school. *Intercultural Education*, *32*(4), 446–463. https://doi.org/10.1080/14675986.2021.1893986
Rönnberg, M. (2003). *"Nya medier" – men samma gamla barnkultur? Om det tredje könets lek, lärande och motstånd via TV, video och datorspel*. Filmförlaget.
Sadr, H. (2002). Children in contemporary Iranian cinema: When we were children. In R. Tapper (Ed.), *The new Iranian cinema: Politics, representation and cinema* (pp. 227–237). I.B Tauris
Shams, N. (2022, 25 January). Med vit, okunnig blick på rasifierades verk: Den svenska kulturkritiken hävdar att den är opartisk men alla skriver utifrån sig själva. *Aftonbladet*. www.aftonbladet.se/kultur/a/z7e3o1/med-vit-okunnig-blick-pa-rasifierades-verk
Short, K. G., & Thomas, L. (2011). Developing intercultural understanding through global children's literature. In R. J. Meyer & K. F. Whitmore (Eds.), *Reclaiming reading: Teachers, students, and researchers regaining spaces for thinking and action* (pp. 149–166). Routledge.
Sissoko, C. O. (Director). (1986). *Nyamanton* [Film]. Centre national de production cinématographique du Mali.
Sommer, D. (2005). *Barndomspsykologi: Utveckling i en förändrad värld* (2nd ed.). Stockholm: Liber.
Sommer, D., Pramling Samuelsson, I., & Hundeide, K. (2010). *Child's perspectives and children's perspectives in theory and practice*. Springer. https://doi.org/10.1007/978-90-481-3316-1

Sutton-Smith, B. (1997). *The ambiguity of play*. Harvard University Press.
Unkrich, L., & Molina, A. (Directors). (2017). *Coco* [Film]. Walt Disney Pictures/ Pixar Animation Studios.
Vázquez-Zentella, V., García, T., & Arceo (2017). Role-play as a pedagogical tool for intercultural education. In R. Cortina (Ed.), *Indigenous education policy, equity, and intercultural understanding in Latin America* (pp. 53–71). Palgrave Macmillan.
Walton, J., Priest, N., & Paradies, Y. (2013). Identifying and developing effective approaches to foster intercultural understanding in schools. *Intercultural Education*, *24*(3), 181–194. https://doi.org/10.1080/14675986.2013.793036
Wells. K. (2021). *Childhood in a global perspective* (3rd ed.). Polity Press.

3 Interculturality, race and inequality in early years

Heidi Layne

Introduction

Daycare centers, playgrounds, as well as schools are places for children to experience friendships across races[1] and to meet people from outside their own family circles. In this way children experience interculturality in their lives almost on a daily basis. This is also where children ask questions and can be curious about *diversity* whether it is about people who look different from them or the environment and nature. Against common belief, children do see race and ethnic diversity, and start to recognize differences and similarities at a very early age (Robinson & Diaz, 2006). That's also when they start asking questions. Teachers, educators and parents play an important role in how children learn to respond to interculturality and in the way they deal with inequalities related to humans and non-human subjects. It is thus important to recognize when interaction and discussions with children lead to constructive understanding of interculturality and when they turn exclusive, leading to discrimination (Layne & Teng, 2022). If a child's natural curiosity is silenced due to sensitivity issues in the adult world, or teachers do not know how to respond to their behaviors, children may learn to shy away from the people and/or objects they are curious about.

In order to problematize children and interculturality, I feel that it is useful and vital to understand how different socio-cultural contexts function and the different terms used to discuss interculturality in these contexts, arguing that contexts and curricula affect the way we understand the world. In this chapter, I thus offer examples from the literature, experiences from Singapore and research from Finland, to help teachers recognize and respond to interculturality, with a focus on inequalities. Examples of policies are also presented to show how inequalities are socially constructed. Many education systems (e.g., Finland), value equality on a policy level. For example, in the Finnish curriculum framework for early childhood education, it is mentioned that racism is unacceptable (Finnish National Agency for

Education, 2014, 2018). However, for the system to be socially just and antiracist, we need to understand how people experience it *within* the system. In the Finnish context, the curriculum framework does not provide guidance on recognizing racism nor on how to discuss racism with children. Preconditions for racism and social exclusion rely on race-thinking and on categorizing people solely by being associated to certain countries, ethnicities, minority groups or by just being 'immigrants' in some cases (Gilroy, 1998). Beliefs, attitudes, values and behaviors that racialize and differentiate between social groups are based on physical and cultural characteristics, geographical locations, or through speaking certain languages, being affiliated to specific religions, or having certain ethnic customs and traditions. This type of thinking may work to privilege the majority and to discriminate against and disadvantage specific races/ethnic minorities (Gilroy, 1998; Lentin, 2004). This chapter presents the examples of Singapore and Finland and how race and racialization as preconditions affect the way in which inequalities and interculturality are understood and presented in policies, early childhood education curricula frameworks and, to some extent, in practice. The case studies used in this chapter are different in nature, but both are based on lived experiences of researching interculturality in education in the two countries.

Why should we talk about inequalities with children?

It is much easier to talk about equality than to recognize and admit the faults of a given system and society. Race talk and racialization processes take place in different forms around the world, and are often tied to social categories such as minority or majority in terms of race, language, sexual orientation, social class, etc. However, it is impossible to claim that any system is equal anywhere in the world, as it depends on whose perspective and whose knowledge and values are predominant in a given curriculum. In each society, a certain type of 'Man' is positioned to represent the majority – as the universal measure of all things – defining the curriculum mostly by what is included and excluded in this rational self-representation (Braidotti, 2002). For education to be more meaningful, I propose a type of early childhood education that recognizes racializing processes and their effects from an early stage as a central part of interculturality. Robinson and Diaz (2006) claim that children do not fully understand the issues of cultural and racial identities even though they recognize that they look different, which may lead to normative discourses on whiteness and racializing practices. A mere focus on language and cultural understanding in the curriculum often disregards the racial identity of children (Layne, 2019).

Curricula are not neutral and they often follow certain types of knowledge traditions and promote certain types of cultural heritage and knowledge. Inequalities are often defined in terms of outcomes and opportunities. The outcome approach has often led to the idea that if you work hard, you can still succeed. Free education for all has been set as one of the parameters for the UNESCO Sustainable Development Goals, Education for All (SDG4) goals. Free education often suggests that success comes with hard work, but in some cases, children still have no access to early childhood education, private tuition and/or extra-curricular activities. In the 1970s, Amartya Sen's (1970a, 1970b) capability framework introduced the idea of evaluating education through human wellbeing to complement the idea of outcome measurements as a quality criterion in education. Sen promoted the idea of understanding the diverse opportunities available for having the freedom to choose and to act (capabilities), including an individual's age, gender, family background and potential disability. Additional elements include climatic conditions, societal conditions (health care, education systems, prevalence of crime, community relationships), customs and convention, among other factors (Sen, 1999, p. 70). Children are born in societies with a specific state of socio-cultural-materialistic values in terms of human rights, climate change and democracy (Gadamer, 1999). Sen (1999) has also discussed successful societies and referred to China as one example of how basic education and health have been organized for all, which is impacting further on her positive economic development while India pays a high prize for inequalities because education and health are not yet accessible to all.

But beyond access to education, schools can prepare children for literacy skills, critical understanding of the world and more academic oriented activities. However, we should not forget that education can be oriented toward life skills too. As such, children come to school with diverse backgrounds, some are more prepared and pressured for academic success, whereas others have gained a lot of practical knowledge through navigating life with maybe less parental guidance or pressure. Different countries have slightly different societal values behind what it means to be *an educated person*, and children do not start their education pathways from equal standings. Singapore and Finland are good examples of societies with well-established education systems but with rather different approaches in (early childhood) education and, overall, in understanding childhoods.

I would also like to discuss some structural inequalities here. Our identities are constructed on the basis of different social categories that impact the way in which we feel either included or excluded from others. These categories are based on (among others) socio-economic backgrounds, race and ethnicity, resulting in racial inequity taking place when two or more racial groups are not standing on an equal footing (Gilroy, 1998). In an ideal world, every education system should include understanding of interculturality as antiracism to advocate racial equity. This can be done through instituting pedagogies, methodologies, and curricula dealing with race awareness of inequities in and out of schools (Layne & Teng, 2022). Antiracism is a political discourse, as well as an intellectual and practical commitment to challenging racism. As a political discourse, antiracism is informed by anti-essentialist understandings of race. This understanding challenges the constructions and understanding of race as a naturalized social hierarchy based on biological difference. Antiracism challenges historically established racist power structures, which, while taking power from some other living species, simultaneously awards power and privilege to others, to serve the interest of those with power (Gilroy, 1998). In this chapter, interculturality is introduced through an antiracist lens.

Schools can also be an arena for reproducing racist ideas. This might take place in the forms of how curricula, learning materials and educators recognize diversity and questioning the very meaning of diversity. Diversity can mean embracing difference through international celebrations, built on a highly nationalistic education value. Or curricula and the learning environment can include activities where children are made to act and think about structural inequalities in terms of opportunities and their actions toward other people and non-human subjects. While diversity is often embraced and celebrated, fewer antiracism programs are included in curricula in some parts of the world.

In what follows, first, I wish to reflect a bit on the curriculum in general. The two case studies explain how interculturality takes diverse lenses in different parts of the world. Finland and Singapore are used as examples in exploring these elements in curricula and practices (among others).

Curricula as systems of knowing

Curricula determine the way in which education is set to transmit certain ways of understanding the world. We are educated to know and reflect on the world through specific lenses. The important question for early childhood educators is to reflect on *whose family traditions, knowledge systems* and *voices* dominate curricula and plan educational activities. Minorities and indigenous people's knowledges are overlooked in most education systems. Edward Said (1995) has written about the way in which European knowledge became 'normalized' at the expense of the exotic other. He demonstrated that, with racial classification, came a centering of European knowledge. Similarly, the classification systems used in science, and given legitimacy and 'naturalness' in educational textbooks, do not consider the cultural context from which they originated. Western scientific worldviews are based on facts gained in controlled environments such as labs, often disconnected from their origins. Besides science is developed from the understanding of people living in a given environment, which does not necessarily apply to other environments and living conditions (Sparkes & Piercey, 2015).

An example of Eurocentrism is found in Carl Linnaeus's development of a system of understanding nature, *Systema Naturae*, first published in 1735 for plants and animals. In this system 'Man' was categorized as an animal. Different races were categorized through skin colors, medical temperaments, physical traits, behaviors, manners of clothing and forms of government. For example, Europeans (*Europaeus*) were white, sanguine, muscular, wise, inventor, covered with tight clothes and governed by rites. Africans (*Africanus*) were described as Black, phlegmatic, lazy, dark hair with many twisted braids, sly, sluggish, neglectful and governed by choice (Linnaeus, 1792, see also www.linnean.org/learning/who-was-linnaeus/linnaeus-and-race). This did not only invent biological races but also a system for racism. My chapter started by explaining how a system of racism is constructed whereby preconditions for racism and social exclusion are race-thinking (Gilroy, 1998). These built-in systems of knowing become invisible and while we try to solve everyday issues occurring among children, we ignore the fact that there are built in systems reproducing inequalities as we try to unpack them. Goulet and Goulet (2014) have explained that the very theories of teaching and learning, for example, are embedded in Eurocentric thinking, leaving out the diverse, rich ways in which Indigenous peoples have known about their world for millennia.

In a framework for educating future planetary citizenship, Andreotti (2021) has proposed to rethink interculturality in education *otherwise* (Andreotti, 2021; see also Dervin, 2015). This raises the importance of moving away from singular, universal beliefs of knowledge toward listening and including counter narratives and knowledges into the curriculum. Furthermore, education should be about dialogue as well as sharing struggles and diverse historical, political and knowledge foundations (Andreotti, 2021; Dervin, 2015; Freire, 1973).

Case study 1: Finland

Policy environment

The Finnish Constitution, section 6 states in regard to equality that everyone is equal before the law. No one shall, without any acceptable reason, be treated differently from other persons on the ground of sex, age, origin, language, religion, conviction, opinion, health, disability or any other reason that concerns his or her person. Children shall also be treated equally, as individuals, and they shall be allowed to influence matters pertaining to themselves to a degree corresponding to their level of development.

Act on Early Childhood Education and Care (540/2018). In 2018 Finland implemented a new Act on Early Childhood Education and Care which states that early childhood education and care aims to: 1) promote the holistic growth, development, health and wellbeing of every child according to the child's age and development; 2) support the conditions for the child's learning and promote lifelong learning and the implementation of equality in education; 3) carry out versatile pedagogical activities based on the child's play, physical activity, arts and cultural heritage, and enable positive learning experiences; 4) ascertain that the child's early childhood education and care environment fosters development and learning and is healthy and safe; 5) safeguard an approach that respects children and ensure that the interpersonal relationships between the children and the early childhood education and care staff are as stable and longstanding as possible; 6) provide all children with equal opportunities for early childhood education and care, promote parity and gender equality, and help the children develop their capacity to understand and respect the general cultural heritage and each other's linguistic, cultural, religious and ideological background; 7) recognize the child's need for individual support and provide the child with appropriate support in early childhood education and care, including support involving multi-professional cooperation where necessary; 8) develop the child's interpersonal and interaction skills, promote the child's ability to act in a peer group, and guide the child toward ethically responsible and sustainable action, respect of other people and membership of society; 9) ensure that the children can participate in and influence matters concerning them; 10) act together with the child and the child's parents or other persons who have custody of the child for the benefit of the child's balanced development and holistic wellbeing, and support the parents or other persons who have custody of the child in their task of bringing up the child.

The National Curriculum Framework Development and Early Childhood Education. In the 1996 National Board of Education document, the Declaration of Human Rights, the Declaration of Children's Rights and the Principle of Sustainable Global Development were explicitly mentioned as starting points of the national curriculum in Finland (cf. National Board of Education (NBE), 1996, p. 8). In the 2000 version of the document this international perspective was overtaken by a national focus: Basic values of Finnish society and national legislation were mentioned as primary starting points. International declarations and conventions were no longer explicitly identified in the following curriculum (see NBE, 2000, p. 7; see also Lappalainen, 2009).

Finnish education policies have a history of promoting internationalization, global and sustainable education as well the Universal Declaration of Human Rights (1948). In addition, the Finnish early childhood education policies are inclusive of the UN convention on the Rights of the Child (1989). However, Finnish curricula are normative in nature providing provide little guidance as to what these mean in practice. Some evidence can be found from research on how democracy and equality are interpreted in early childhood education. In their study Hellman et al. (2018) interviewed principals, teachers and parents (with an immigrant background) in the Nordic countries (Finland, Sweden, Norway and Iceland) to understand how they felt about the implementation of these values. They were merely interpreted as making every child visible and taking care of and helping each other.

With increasing immigration in the 1990s the notion of diversity has become a synonym for ethnic and cultural difference in Finnish Early Childhood Education and Care (ECEC) (Layne & Dervin, 2016; Layne & Lipponen, 2014; Millei, 2019). The increase in ethnic diversity pushed for the need for multicultural education and research on teaching children with diverse cultural and language backgrounds. However, there have always been diversities in Finnish society: different religious backgrounds, people with different family and social circumstances, as well as different languages, gender and sexualities, among others (see Dervin's notion of *diverse diversities* in opposition to mere diversity, Dervin, 2014). In addition, Finland has always had national minority students, such as Sámi from Lapland and Roma children. Considering this gap in recognizing these inherent aspects of diversity in Finnish society, being a Finn remains to a large extent related to whiteness (Layne, 2019).

Everyday practices of interculturality in Finland

Putting interculturality into practice is a process through which educators apply cognitive knowledge, understand the links between inequalities and different social categories (race, ethnicity, language, language hierarchies, gender, sexuality, minority) and promote behaviors and actions leading to acknowledge and decrease inequalities (Stein & Andreotti, 2021). An intercultural curriculum is for everyone, not only for *immigrants* or *minorities*. The Finnish curriculum emphasizes interculturality in terms of cultural and linguistic diversity, human rights, sustainable development goals for education, equality and democracy. However, based on a survey conducted on everyday quality of early childhood education done by the National Education Evaluation Centre in Finland (2019), interculturality and diversities appeared to be neglected in early education. The Report of the Non-Discrimination Ombudsman, *Racism and Discrimination – Everyday Experiences for People of African Descent in Finland* (2018), indicates that racism exists at all levels of education, starting in early childhood education.

In what follows, I focus on nine Finnish kindergarten teachers who were interviewed and asked to send pictures to describe how they experience interculturality and everyday racism in Finnish kindergartens. This was part of a study on everyday multiculturalism and everyday racism in Finnish early childhood education. The kindergartens were located in the Helsinki metropolitan area, in neighborhoods with relatively large numbers of immigrant families. However, my interest goes beyond 'immigrant families' here.

Everyday interculturality

One Finnish teacher made the following statement when talking about every day practices working with children with diverse backgrounds: 'Each child has a right to be challenged on their individual level'. In general, everyday interculturality was recognized in planning the activities through language support for children whose home language is different from the school language, in this case the Finnish language. Teachers use pictures to illustrate daily activities and for example the type of clothes that children need to wear for playing outdoors (see Figure 3.1). In Finland, due to the weather

Figure 3.1 Examples of how pictures with Finnish words are used to support children who are learning the Finnish language for daily routines. Photos by author.

conditions, children need a variety of clothes for different types of weather when attending early childhood education. This can be also challenging for low-income families.

Besides language support, teachers talked about interculturality through friendships. Friendships are often formed based on language and development levels, as well as gender. Arvola et al. (2020) reported that children with diverse language backgrounds were found to be more involved especially in rule play, but they were less participative in role play. Children in Finland are usually considered as active agents and composers of meaningful learning experiences through play in early childhood pedagogy. The authors suggest that teachers in Finland could pay specific attention to the involvement of children with an immigrant background to learning activities, specifically to play-based interventions and to shared cultural creation, where language is one important aspect to consider (Arvola et al., 2020, p. 11). The teachers I interviewed, mentioned the importance of adult presence and guidance when children navigate friendships. An example was mentioned by a teacher: they noticed that no one had memorized the name of one of these children. As a solution, they planned activities to better include this child with other children. The teacher also mentioned methods like friendship trees and drawings used to pair and group children for play activities (see Figure 3.2).

One teacher also mentioned how she had experienced children as young as under three years old, choosing not to play with friends of darker skin colors. Since children are at times explicit about their opinions and the way in which they express them, early childhood education would be fruitful stage for antiracism actions. One way of diversifying the learning materials in Finland in terms of racial representations has been to add Black baby dolls in housekeeping corners for children to play with. Based on research and conversations with early childhood teachers, these baby dolls have been mistreated by children (Layne & Lipponen, 2014). The same topic was discussed by one teacher I interviewed: 'I remember some time ago in the outdoor activities, there was a dark-skinned baby doll . . . and I remember that it was treated fairly bad . . . so young children felt alienated from so dark-skinned dolls . . . the doll was there out of good will, but it led to counter reactions'. Finnish early childhood pedagogy relies on play as the main mean for learning. At the same time, children's play episodes seem to reproduce the system of power that exists in the larger social system. To respond to the need to diversify learning materials, one teacher shared pictures of clothes teachers sewed for baby dolls made from fabric that some parents had donated (see Figure 3.3).

Teachers discussed the shortage of learning materials available to represent the variety of food objects in the housekeeping area and the types of clothes children wear. Housekeeping corners and play areas, still today,

Interculturality, race and inequality in early years 85

Figure 3.2 Friendship tree (Ystävyyden puu). The word *friend* is translated in the languages of the children. Name tags with the names of the children are tagged to the tree for grouping purposes. Photo by author.

often represent the old-fashioned type of Finnish countryside home with wooden furniture. The teachers select the teaching aids and materials from catalogs provided by specific private companies, which contain very few diversified entries.

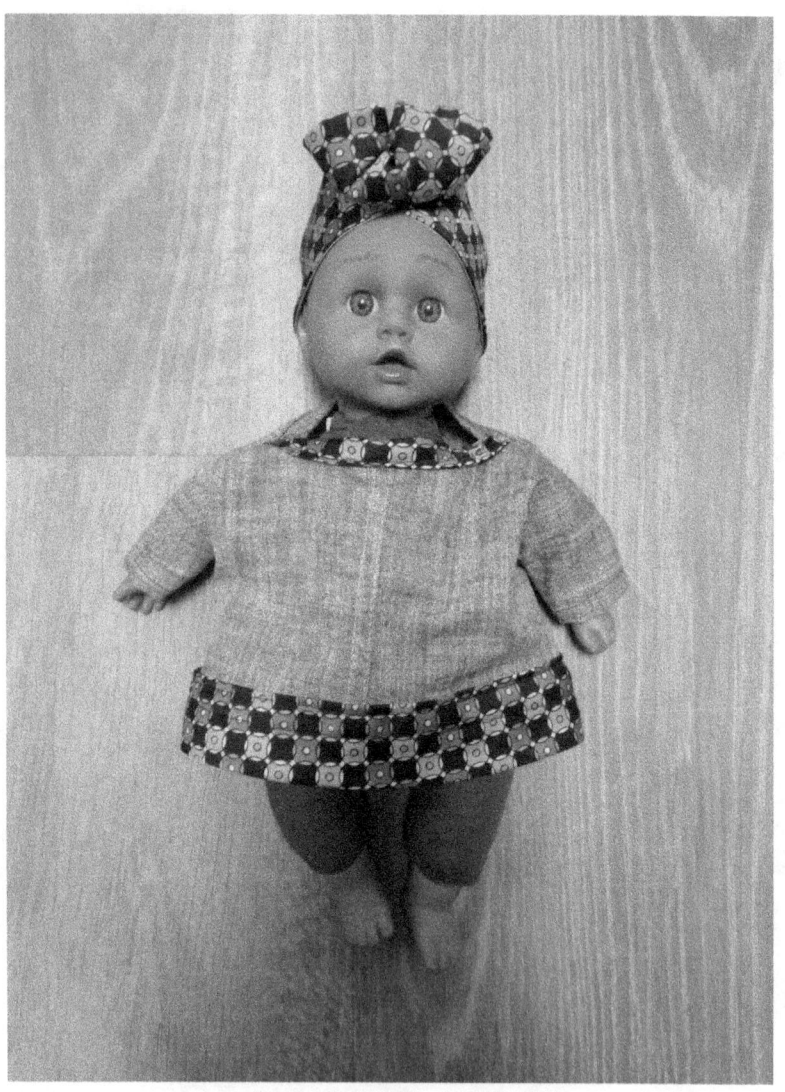

Figure 3.3 Examples of self-made clothes for baby dolls from fabric donated by parents. Photos by author.

While some teachers recognize the risk of exoticism of everyday interculturality, if diversity is tied to cultural diversity (mainly geographical or religious cultures), others still talked about Africans, African features and languages, as if it were *one country*, and something

Interculturality, race and inequality in early years 87

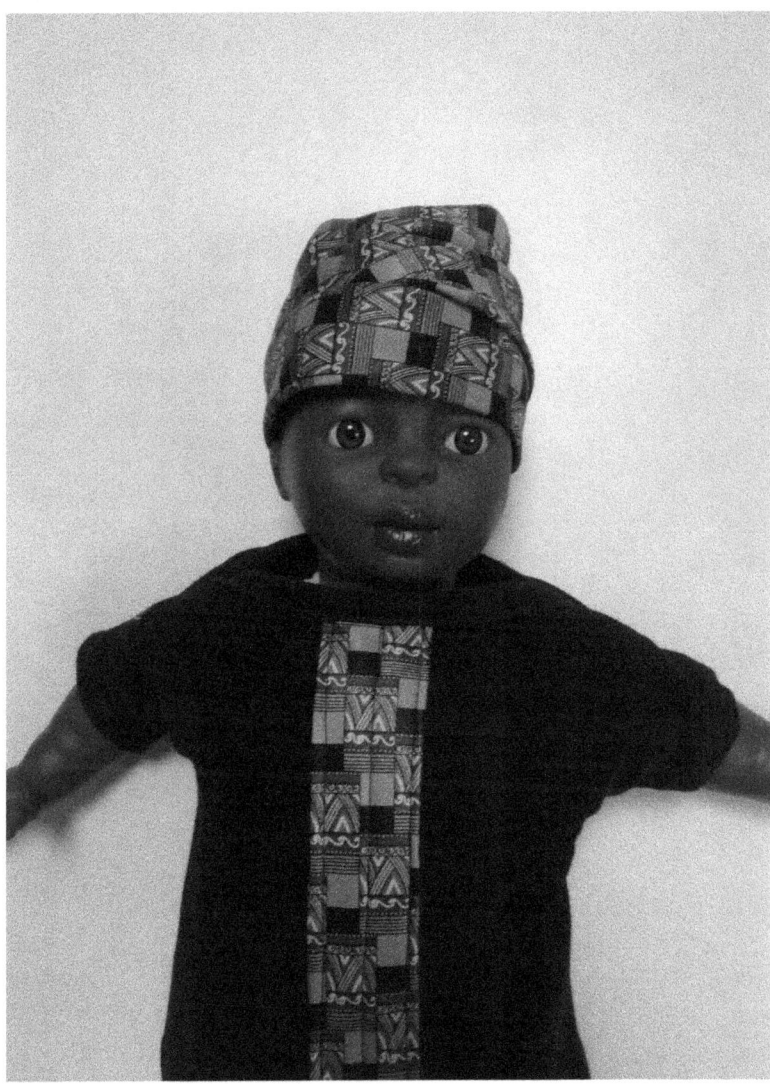

Figure 3.3 (Continued)

very distant and exotic (in a positive tone though). One nice and easy way to present diversity in the classroom is to ask children to create their self-portraits based on their own desired identity markers in terms of gender and other aspects depicted in the clothing that they draw (see Figure 3.4).

Figure 3.4 Self-portrait of a young learner representing diversity. Photo by author.

Lastly, some teachers were able to recognize the role of norms in education and how norms vary across different life experiences. At the same time, the annual planning in the Finnish early childhood education is based on the Christian calendar and celebrations and public holidays common for

Christian traditions. This norm is yet barely recognized, leaving many children and families without proper recognition of their own celebrations.

Talking about race and racism

The teachers approached diversity and racism from multiple perspectives. Overall findings indicate that teachers don't know how to talk about racism. They also mentioned the lack of systematic approach to interculturality and antiracism in teacher education and training. Teachers do not know how to talk about it with young children either and appear to be unaware of age-appropriate practices. This might be due to the sensitivity of race talk, and also the fact that teachers in Finland are predominantly White, with structural racism being unknown in their daily experiences. The curriculum framework for early childhood education mentions racism in one sentence: '*racism is not accepted*'. This does not necessarily guide teachers to become antiracist in terms of acting against racism and inequalities. To be antiracist, one needs to act against racism. Witnessing without action and recognition does not lead to promote interculturality and antiracism pedagogy. Some teachers did mention talking about racism if the children initiated a conversation about it. However, I argue that advocating interculturality needs to be proactive not mere reactions to events that have already happened – and when harm is already done. A myth seems to exist among the interviewed educators: if one represents families and children in schools (by, for example, posting pictures of diverse families on a wall), hostility toward others and minorities would automatically disappear. Surveys and quality measures in (early childhood) education in Finland show otherwise. Although 'No to Racism' signs and campaigns won't solve the issue of racism, and neither will an annual antiracism week promoting antiracism activities, these types of activities could raise some conversations among children, teachers and parents.

Teachers should not be left alone, and it should not be an individual choice to promote antiracism or not. Antiracism should become a joint act involving what to take away from curricula and the whole education community, including parents.

Case study 2: Singapore

Singapore is often described as a small nation without natural resources, where education is important as the society is dependent on its skilled people for economic survival and development (Gopinathan, 2001). The population consists of Chinese Singaporeans (74.1%, with Chinese Mandarin as recognized mother tongue), Malay Singaporeans (13.4%, Malay as mother tongue) and Singaporean Indians (9.2%, with Tamil as mother tongue). In addition, some people belong to the category of Others 3.3% with diverse languages not available in public schools. Children get some mother tongue tuition at school as their chosen mother tongue (Chinese Mandarin, Malay, or Tamil), where English is the language of instruction, as a reminder of the times when Singapore was a British colony. It is important to bear in mind that Singapore is also a multireligious society, recognizing different religious celebrations.

Singapore is considered as an international hub and as a gate between East and West. Children are by no means separate from the economic powers and from assessment-oriented education values in Singapore. Besides, Singapore values a system of meritocracy, meaning that the responsibility is placed on the individual to work hard and succeed, without recognizing that not everyone has the same opportunities, as was discussed earlier in this chapter (see Teo, 2018). The government of Singapore has a strong desire to provide more opportunities for good quality early childhood education for the diverse population in the country. The 2003 implemented and 2012 revised curriculum framework (*NEL*) aimed to promote sustainable, lifelong learning instead of anticipating an academic-focused pedagogy in kindergartens.

In recent years, the government has also put a lot of emphasis on promoting opportunities for children with a low-income background to attend better quality early childhood education. Confucian education, which is often regarded as grounding philosophy for the Singaporean education system, considers individuals in relation to others and to their society (Ho, 2018). However, as a multicultural society with Malays being natives to the island, and Indians being another minority group besides the Chinese Singaporean majority, not all Singaporeans necessarily relate to this understanding of 'Confucianism' (a term in English that encompasses different perspectives, beyond *Confucius* himself and that has no real equivalent in Chinese), leaving beliefs of minorities less recognized.

The NEL Curriculum framework adopts an idea of children as unique persons who construct their own knowledge, skills and dispositions. Moreover, NEL applies specific learning areas including: (a) aesthetics and creative learning; (b) discovery of the world; (c) language and literacy; (d) motor skills development; (e) numeracy; and (f) social and emotional skills. In addition, the document lists some learning dispositions such as perseverance, reflectiveness, appreciation, inventiveness, a sense of wonder, curiosity and engagement. NEL has also a section for mother tongue instruction (NEL, 2012).

The emphasis on meritocracy has shaped the implemented curriculum of Singapore's education system – one that focuses on content, assessment and achievement (Gopinathan, 2001). A type of education system that values meritocracy does not recognize skills that many children and young people adopt in the low-income families, such as capacity for care and 'indigenous' knowledge (Teo, 2018). Children with low-income family backgrounds also have less opportunities to take part in extra curricular activities and private tuition that are common for preschool-age children in Singapore.

In Singapore, meritocracy can be interpreted as follows:

> Our unified national education system provides equal opportunities for each student to learn and to achieve his or her potential. Meritocracy recognizes and rewards everyone who works hard and excels. Meritocracy is highly compatible with the multiracial model of society, as its very essence lies in allowing all races to advance in whatever field, solely on the basis of achievement, merit and hard work. In the sociological literature, meritocracy is widely recognized as a system for sorting, selecting, and then differentially rewarding people based on narrow notions of what is worth rewarding and what is not
>
> (Teo, 2018, p. 31).

Racial harmony as state initiative and education toward tolerance

Singapore is a multiracial society that embraces harmony. Multiculturalism is a core element of this centralized educational system, which consists of policies such as the National Education and the National Shared Values frames (Ho, 2018). These value frameworks include racial and religious harmony and contain values such as *harmony, consensus* and *national unity* (Ho, 2018; Ministry of Education, 2007). Harmony is maintained through policies where the racial categories of Chinese, Malays, Indian and Others (CMIO) are used. Harmony has been criticized by scholars for silencing voices and unifying histories, rather than allowing multiple narratives of Singapore (Ho, 2018). As a multicultural society, Singapore is often portrayed as an example of racial harmony and as a place with zero tolerance for racism and conflicts. However, there is little recognition of the minority-majority power imbalance in the political system and everyday life. For example, Malays underperform in terms of educational achievement (e.g., earning of higher education degrees) and economic indicators (median monthly household income) (see Chew, 2018). The Singapore Constitution guarantees that all persons are equal before the law and that there shall be no discrimination on the basis of, among others things, race. In addition, the Government has the responsibility to care constantly for the interests of racial and religious minorities.

The framework under which racial harmony has been celebrated goes back to riots that broke out in 1964. In 1997, the Ministry of Education marked July 21st as Racial Harmony Day. This established an ontology of conflict avoidance that may impact the ways racial harmony is taught and discussed. Racial Harmony Day is a day during which preschools and schools reflect on and celebrate Singapore's success as a racially harmonious nation and a society built on a rich diversity of culture and heritage. On this day, in preschools and schools across the nation, students are encouraged to dress in their traditional costumes. Traditional delicacies are also featured in the celebrations; traditional games are played in schools; and further inter-class competitions are sometimes organized. Racial Harmony Day is also discussed in the media annually as the following collection of themes reflects from the national newspaper called *The Strait Times* (2017) in celebration of the 20th Anniversary of National Harmony Day:

1) CELEBRATING TOGETHER: Exchanging greetings and celebrating such occasions together will show that everyone has a place in one another's festivals and help cement ties among the various races and unite our people.
2) OPPORTUNITIES TO PRACTICE RACIAL HARMONY: PLAYGROUND TIME: The time mothers spend accompanying their children to school and waiting for them to be dismissed offers many opportunities to build friendships with other mums and children of other races.
3) FOCUS ON YOUNGSTERS: For racial harmony to prevail today, when issues such as Islamophobia occasionally arise, it is important to focus on the young. Educating them about cultural sensitivity can go a long way.' (www.straitstimes.com/singapore/racial-harmony-day-in-singapore-20-years-on)

Singapore considers itself as a shining example of race relations. This has added greatly to the country's stability. Racial Harmony Day is about celebrating different foods, festivals and fashions, but it can also be criticized for its simplistic presentation of cultures (Ho, 2018; Mardiana et al., 2021). Earlier research shows that such celebrations may help students to understand each other's cultures but does not tackle the more complex issues of racism and bullying in schools and in the wider society.

Racial identity and racial relations in schools and beyond

In a multicultural and postcolonial society like Singapore, language and its hierarchies are also a way to maintain minority-majority power imbalance. There is strong evidence that a foundation in spoken language competence is important for academic achievement, as well as social and emotional competence (Duff & Tomblin, 2018). For young children in Singapore, the language environment both in and outside their home is essential in shaping their language profiles and competencies before they begin primary school (Cheng, 2020). Additionally, socio-economic status is connected to home language use in Singapore, with a higher percentage of children from lower socio-economic backgrounds reporting their mother tongues as being the dominant language used at home while children with higher educated parents and with more middle-class background tend to use English at home. Mardiana et al. (2021) discovered in their study on how young Singaporeans navigate diversities, that language is used as a mean for including and excluding peers at schools. A rather common practice in Singapore is that early childhood education providers promote and advertise bilingual learning experiences in Chinese Mandarin and English, leaving children with other mother tongues with less attention during the preschool years. This can be quite problematic, specifically for children with a minority and low-income family background, with less access to learning in their own mother tongue. Such practices can directly contribute to the underachievement of learners with a minority language background such as Malay children in schools.

Experiences of race represent a significant part of how adults and children identify self and others in Singapore. From birth, filling out official forms, already in the first-grade, means being identified in the system based on the racial categories of CMIO. Race is a biological category in Singapore but it becomes a social construct when navigating through different experiences of race relations. Through my personal experience of living in Singapore I noticed that even the appointment card for the medical clinic indicates people's race. Furthermore, local TV-channels are referred to as *the Malay channel, English Channel, Indian channel* (Lee et al., 2004, p. 116). Lee et al. (2004), in their study on race relations in Singapore schools, observed how groupings in schools often go by race and gender. Children may engage in encounters with friends from diverse backgrounds in schools. And yet, for example, the food stalls in the school canteens are based on the ethnic divisions of Malay, Chinese, Indian, Western food, where children line up based on their own background. In my own experience, when visiting day care centers, sometimes, I was asked by children if I was Malay or English (I am a white Finn).

Multiculturalism is a norm in Singapore and therefore race talk is a very typical topic of conversation, however, the topics of racism and racial discrimination are considered rather sensitive. The idea of harmony is to tolerate and avoid topics that can create disagreements and conflicts. Therefore, racism and antiracism pedagogy are challenging topics for teachers to deal with. This was also young people's experiences in Mardiana et al. (2021) and Layne and Teng (2022).

Despite racial and religious harmony, an increasing number of racial conflicts have been portrayed in the media. Two recent incidents indicate that 'minoritizing' still exists. In July 2019 Dennis Chew, a Singaporean Chinese actor, appeared in an ad campaign for a nationwide cashless payment initiative representing each ethnic group, with darkened skin to feature Indians in Singapore. Later, the advertisement was removed, and was admitted being inappropriate. Two local artists came up with a rap song featuring this incident, and their overall experiences of being a minority (Singaporean Malays) in Singapore. There were many apologies by different instances involved in the episode, but in the end, the rap song was perceived as a threat to harmony by the government, and an official warning was issued while the producers of the advertisement got away with an apology.

Another recent example is a bullying incident from March 2020. Education Minister Ong Ye Kung stood up in Facebook after the bullying of a Malay girl in a majority Chinese Singaporean School went public. Besides Facebook, *The Strait Times* reported the issue on 11.3.2020. A group of pupils at the school had picked on a Malay classmate and written her 'nasty' notes. The Minister took a stand arguing that bullying was wrong and could not be tolerated anywhere, especially in schools. The case came to light when the bullied girl's brother posted on Twitter the notes that she had received from her classmates. The school had only a handful of Malays, and the girl had been called names and cyber-bullied. The comments on the Minister's Facebook page encouraged many people to share about bullying and discrimination.

Conclusion: *Toward play for interculturality?*

This chapter aimed to demonstrate how intercultural encounters and inequalities are presented and discussed in similar and different terms in two contexts: Finland and Singapore. Socio-cultural contexts matter in education, and since there is no universal way of understanding interculturality, we need different lenses and paradigms to interpret this world and childhoods. Both countries, Singapore and Finland, have adopted rather 'soft' approaches to interculturality policy-wise. In Finland, cultural and language diversity are emphasized while in Singapore racial and religious harmony is the main focus. In Singapore, harmony and sensitivity to talk about racism seem to prevent teachers from applying antiracism pedagogy. Eurocentrism, referring to Western ways of understanding the world, permeates the education system at all levels in Finland. In Singapore the current debate revolves around the Anglo-Chinese Singaporean majority and, for example, debates about so-called Confucian values and whose history and what traditions are studied in schools and are visible in the play and learning environment in early childhood education settings.

In Finland, due to equality being taken for granted, teachers lack tools and vocabulary to apply an antiracism pedagogy to understand racism. In Singapore, race and language hierarchies, as well as social class systems, are part of structural categories that predominate the way in which inequalities are constructed and experienced in everyday life. Lim (2016) brought to attention how early childhood educators need to be prepared to discuss social justice issues with children. She used the example of observed role play in a preschool in Singapore. *Domestic helper* was the role that was given to one child but they refused to play that role (Lim, 2016). Housing, schooling and other policies are based on dividing the small island state's population into racial categories. With religious harmony, the state recognizes different faith-based celebrations. Racial and religious harmony is meant to teach children to live side by side with people from diverse beliefs systems and with varying worldviews. However, these worldviews may be merely tolerated rather than accepted as a part of the school curriculum and practices. Finland recognizes mainly Christian celebrations and religious education is part of the national curriculum. Unlike Singapore, Finland includes racism and antiracism as topics in schools. In the Western media, specifically social media, these conversations often take directions toward hate speech without any political control in the way they are discussed. This has had unpleasant consequences leading to racist experiences. Yet, there is not enough support for antiracism pedagogy through Finnish policies or in teacher education.

Moving toward the end of this chapter, what I suggest here is that understanding how diverse socio-cultural contexts shape childhoods and experiences represent an important part of interculturality in early childhood education. Education tends to create hegemonies and national narratives that become norms that we all accept (invisibly). Interculturality in education has a role to play in making these invisible norms visible and in questioning them. We were not born in a world that is created by us, but in a world that was and is constructed by others (Arendt, 1958). As educators and policy-makers, we can work with children and families to create new worlds or worldviews. One way of initiating this is to provide safe space and vocabulary in schools to discuss and negotiate daily experiences of racism and discrimination. This also needs to be visible in curricula and in daily planning.

Freire (1970/1993) introduced the notion of consciousness in pedagogical thinking that incorporated the experiences and reflections of everyone involved, thereby promoting joint decision-making and autonomy within the educational process. This educational stance requires educators to be willing to listen to and foster relationships with students, through dialogue and collaboration, in order to make decisions. Furthermore, in allowing children to express themselves and using their input in making decisions, children and their families understand that they can, in fact, be leaders of change in their schools and in their community (MacBeath, 2006). Play may also be a way for teachers to understand children and for children to express their experiences and conceptual understanding of the world. From a postmodern perspective, children are seen as knowledgeable, competent, strong and powerful members of society (Bruner, 1996). Talking to one preschool teacher in Singapore during the COVID-19 circuit breaker home-based learning period, she mentioned that the concern was that parents let their children just play or watch something on their phones. This is not an uncommon comment about *play* in the Singapore context. Recent research shows that play indeed requires social competence because play includes active carrying out of negotiations and agreements between facts and fiction (Kangas et al., 2019). Play is also about negotiating affordances. Therefore, play has been seen as a dynamic and dialogical process in an imaginary environment (Møller, 2015). Through play, children may make sense of life: Children share their lifeworlds with other children and create meanings built upon experiences (Pramling & Pramling-Samuelsson, 2011; Vygotsky, 1978).

Play is vital in (re-)conceptualizing childhood and curricula around the world but it requires sensitivity and preparedness from educators to allow the mixing and socializing that play facilitates to happen. Paramount for intercultural interactions is that the child's experiences and conceptual world are understood and expanded in relationships with other children, educators and learning environments. However, there is also a danger of unintended racism or exclusive discourses if teachers are not sensitive and knowledgeable enough. In Finland play is placed at the center of early learning practices, yet the learning environment does not always reflect and provide affordances for children with diverse backgrounds to feel connected with learning materials. Moreover, play-based pedagogies rarely promote the idea of antiracism, discuss inequalities or provide tools for teachers to implement antiracism pedagogy through play. Children's play is an opportunity for teachers to initiate conversations on the topics of racism and structural inequalities. Can play then be a future tool for antiracism pedagogy in early childhood education as it provides diverse ways of interpreting the world, if allowed and encouraged. As a tool to develop interculturality *otherwise* in early childhood education, I believe that play should be further explored.

Note

1 While rereading each other's chapters, Fred asked me why I use (only) the word 'race' here ('across different races') since many readers might not be used to seeing this concept in relation to interculturality – some might use *ethnicity* or any other ideological substitute. I simply replied that since this chapter is about inequality and racism, 'race-thinking is the foundation for racism'.

References

Andreotti, V. (2021). Depth education and the possibility of GCE otherwise. *Globalisation, Societies and Education*, *19*(4), 496–509. https://doi.org/10.1080/14 767724.2021.1904214

Arendt, H. (1995). *The human condition*. The University of Chicago Press.

Arvola, O., Pankakoski, K., Reunamo, J., & Kyttälä, M. (2020). Culturally and linguistically diverse children's participation and social roles in the Finnish early childhood education – is play the common key? *Early Child Development and Care*, *191*(15), 2351–2363. https://doi.org/10.1080/03004430.2020.1716744

Braidotti, R. (2002). *Metamorphoses: Towards a materialist theory of becoming*. Polity Press/Blackwell.

Bruner, C. (1996). *Realizing a vision for children, families, and neighborhoods: An alternative to other modest proposals*. National Center for Service Integration, Child and Family Policy Center.

Cheng, C. C. (2020). Eye on the future: Diverse family language policy in three Singaporean Malay homes with preschool children. *Asia-Pacific Journal of Research in Early Childhood Education*, *14*(1), 125–147.

Chew, P. K. H. (2018). Racism in Singapore: A Review and recommendations for future research. *Journal of Pacific Rim Psychology*, *12*(5), 1–8. https://doi.org/10.1017/prp.2018.3.

Convention on the rights of the child. (1989). Treaty no. 27531. United Nations Treaty Series, 1577, 3–178.

Dervin, F. (2014). International pre-service teachers' perceptions of experienced teachers' intercultural (in)competence in Finland. *Educational Practice and Theory*, *36*(2), 5–25. https://doi.org/10.7459/ept/36.2.02

Dervin, F. (2015). Towards post-intercultural teacher education: Analysing 'extreme' intercultural dialogue to reconstruct interculturality. *European Journal of Teacher Education*, *38*(1), 71–86. https://doi.org/10.1080/02619768.2014.902441

Duff, D., & Tomblin, J. B. (2018). Literacy as an outcome of language development and its impact on children's psychosocial and emotional development. In R. E. Tremblay, M., Boivin, & RDeV Peters (Eds.). S. Rvachew (Topic ed.).

Encyclopedia of early childhood development [online]. www.child-encyclopedia.com/language-development-and-literacy/accordingexperts/literacy-outcome-language-development-and-its.

Finnish National Agency for Education [Opetushallitus]. (2014). *National core curriculum for pre-primary education 2014*.

Finnish National Agency for Education [Opetushallitus]. (2018). *National core curriculum for early childhood education 2016*.

Freire, P. (1970/1993). *Pedagogy of the oppressed*. M. Ramos (Trans.). The Continuum International Publishing Group Inc.

Gadamer, H.-G. (1999). On the possibility of a philosophical ethics. In H.-G. Gadamer (Ed.), *Hermeneutics, religion and ethics* (J. Weinsheimer, Trans., pp. 18–36). Yale University Press.

Gilroy, P. (1998). Race ends here. *Ethnic and Racial Studies 21*(5), 838–847. https://doi.org/10.1080/014198798329676

Gopinathan, S. 2001. *Globalisation, the state and education policy in Singapore*. In J. Tan, S. Gopinathan, & W. K. Ho (Eds.), *Challenges facing Singapore education system today*, (pp. 3–17). Prentice Hall.

Goulet, L. M., & Goulet, K. N. (2014). *Teaching each other. Nehinuw concepts & indigenous pedagogies*. UBC Press.

Hellman, A., Ragnarsdóttir, H., Jónsdóttir, F. B., Blöndal, H., Lauritsen, K., & Paavola, H. (2018). Socially just learning spaces: Inclusion and participation in preschool settings in the Nordic countries. In H. Ragnarsdóttir & L. A. Kulbrandstad (Eds.), *Learning spaces for inclusion and social justice: Success stories from four Nordic countries*. Cambridge Scholars Publishing.

Ho, L.-C. (2010). "Don't worry, i'm not going to report you": Education for citizenship in Singapore. *Theory & Research in Social Education, 38*(2), 217–247. https://doi.org/10.1080/00933104.2010.10473423

Ho, L.-C. (2018). Consensus not conflict: Harmony and multicultural education in Singapore. In Y.-K. Cha, S.-H. Ham, & M. Lee (Eds.), *Routledge international handbook of multicultural education research in Asia Pacific* (pp. 83–90). Routledge.

Kangas, J., Harju-Luukkainen, H., Brotherus, A., Kuusisto, A., & Gearon, L. (2019). Playing to learn in Finland: Early childhood curricular and operational contexts. In S. Garvis & S. Phillipson (Eds.), *Policification of early childhood education and care: Early childhood education in the 21st Century volume III* (pp. 71–85). Routledge. https://doi.org/10.4324/9780203730539-7

Karila, K. (2008). A Finnish viewpoint on professionalism in early childhood education. *European Early Childhood Education Research Journal, 16*(2), 210–223. https://doi.org/10.1080/13502930802141634

Kulbrandstad, L. A., Layne, H., Paavola, H., Hellman, A., & Ragnarsdóttir, H. (2018). Immigrant students in Nordic educational policy documents. In H. Ragnarsdóttir & L. A. Kulbrandstad (Eds.), *Learning spaces for inclusion and social justice: Success stories from four Nordic countries* (pp. 32–68). Cambridge Scholars Publishing.

Lappalainen, S. (2009). Making differences and reflecting on diversities: Embodied nationality among preschool children. *International Journal of Inclusive Education, 13*(1), 63–78. https://doi.org/10.1080/13603110701273691

Layne, H. (2019). Ethnicity and race in childhood (Finland). *Bloomsbury Education and Childhood Studies*. (Digital resource). https://doi.org/10.5040/9781350934399.029

Layne, H., & Dervin, F. (2016). Problematizing Finland's pursuit of intercultural (kindergarten) teacher education. *Multicultural Education Review*, *8*(2), 118–134. https://doi.org/10.1080/2005615X.2016.1161290

Layne, H., & Lipponen, L. (2014). Student teachers in the contact zone: Developing critical intercultural "teacherhood" in kindergarten teacher education. *Globalisation, Societies and Education*, *14*(1), 110–126. https://doi.org/10.1080/14767724.2014.980780

Layne, H., & Teng, S. S. (2022). Developing intercultural mindedness through an experiential learning activity: A case study from Singapore. *Education Sciences*, *12*(3). https://doi.org/10.3390/educsci12030212

Lee, K. E. C., Cherian, M., Ismail, R., Ng, M., Sim, J., & Chee, M. F. (2004). Children's experiences of multiracial relationships in informal primary school settings. In L. A. Eng (Ed.), *Beyond rituals and riots: Ethnic relations and social cohesion in Singapore* (pp. 114–145). Times Academic Press.

Lentin, A. (2004). *Racism and anti-racism in Europe*. Pluto Press.

Lim, S. (2016). "I have ... do you have?": Facilitating children's play and talk in a consumer society. In M. Waniganayake & M. Ebbeck (Eds.), *Play and pedagogy in early childhood* (2nd ed., pp. 134–146). Oxford University Press.

Linnaeus, C. (1792). *The animal kingdom, or zoological system*. Edited by J. F. Gmelin (Ed.), (Trans. Robert Kerr). A. Strahan, T. Cadell, and W. Creech, 1792.

MacBeath, J. (2006). Finding a voice, finding self. *Educational Review*, *58*(2), 195–207. https://doi.org/10.1080/00131910600584140

Mardiana, A. B., Teng, S. S., Layne, H., & Kaurani, S. N. (2021). Navigating diversities: Experiences of youths in one Singapore school. *Journal of Multicultural Discourses*, *16*(3), 258–276. https://doi.org/10.1080/17447143.2021.1934479

Millei, Z. (2019). Re-orienting and re-acting (to) diversity in Finnish early childhood education and care. *Journal of Early Childhood Education Research*, *8*(1), 47–58.

Ministry of Education (MOE). (2003). *Launch of pre-school curriculum framework*. www.moe.gov.sg/media/press/2003/pr20030120_print.htm

Ministry of Education (MOE). (2013). *Nurturing early learners: A curriculum for kindergartens in Singapore. Educators' guide: overview*. www.moe.gov.sg/docs/defaultsource/document/education/preschool/files/nel/edu/guide/overview.pdf

Møller, S. J. (2015). Imagination, playfulness and creativity in children's play with different toys. *American Journal of Play*, *7*(3), 322–346.

Non-discimination Ombudsman. (2020). https://syrjinta.fi/en/-/report-of-the-non-discrimination-ombudsman-racism-and-everyday-experiences-for-people-of-african-descent-in-finland

Oberhuemer, P. (1994). Stories make a difference: Intercultural dialogue in the early years. *European Early Childhood Education Research Journal*, *2*(1), 35–42. https://doi.org/10.1080/13502939485207511

Opetushallitus. (2016a). www.oph.fi/sites/default/files/documents/esiopetuksen_opetussuunnitelman_perusteet_2014.pdf

Opetushallitus. (2016b). www.oph.fi/sites/default/files/documents/perusopetuksen_opetussuunnitelman_perusteet_2014.pdf

Opetushallitus. (2018). www.oph.fi/sites/dfault/files/documents/varhaiskasvatussuunnitelman_perusteet.pdf

Pramling, N., & Pramling-Samuelsson, I. (2011). *Educational encounters: Nordic studies in early childhood didactics*. Springer.

Robinson, K. H., & Diaz, C. J. (2006). *Diversity and difference in early childhood education: issues for theory and practice*. Open University Press.

Said, E. (1995). *Orientalism: Western conceptions of the Orient*. Penguin Books.

Sen, A. (1970a). The impossibility of a Paretian liberal. *Journal of Political Economy, 78*(1), 152–157.

Sen, A. (1970b). *Collective choice and social welfare*. Holden Day.

Sen, A. (1999). *Development as freedom*. Knopf.

Sparkes, L. L., & Piercey, D. W. (2015). *Indigenous ways of knowing and Western science: Including traditional knowledge in post-secondary biology courses*. Department of Biology, Vanier College.

Stein, S., & Andreotti, V. (2021). Global citizenship otherwise. In E. Bosio (Ed.), *Conversations on global citizenship education: Research, teaching and learning* (pp. 13–36). Routledge.

Teo, Y. Y. (2018). *This is what inequality looks like*. Ethos Books. Universal Declaration of Human Rights (1948).

Vygotsky, L. S. (1978). *Mind in society: The development of higher psychological processes*. Harvard University Press.

Conclusion

Who are the real 'interculturalists'?

A short narrative

Let us start wrapping up with a short narrative. After writing his chapter for this book, Fred remembered another unexpected encounter with a Chinese friend's child (8 years old) from a couple of years ago. While Fred and his friend were working together on a paper, the little girl came into the study for her daily English lesson with the mother [she had just started learning English and had never met a foreigner before]. Using a textbook, the mother made her repeat words such as *frog, table, boy, horse*, etc. Fred was just sitting there working. The little girl was not very motivated and repeated the words in a less than enthusiastic way. When Fred heard the word *panda* in English, he looked at her and repeated the word to her. This started a half-hour playful session that turned the lesson into noisy, funny and happy moments. The little girl asked her mum: '你是"用英语怎么说?'(How do you say 'you are' in English?). She then 'took over' the class. Moving around the study, pointing at objects in the study and referring to some of the words from the textbook, Fred and the little girl started challenging each other: 'you are a table!'; 'you are a pencil!'; 'you are a frog!', 'you are an elephant!', 'you are a boy cat!' . . . Although their interactions were limited to simple structures and words, they both laughed, smiled and enjoyed these moments. Suddenly, in the middle of the brouhaha, the little girl snatched her mother's phone and started showing Fred apps that could transform people into animals, wizards and strange characters. The little girl navigated through the phone without any problem and took selfies with Fred, laughing at every funny picture and continuing with the 'you are a xx' game. At no point during their interaction did the little girl show any sign of anxiety having to talk to someone who was obviously different from her, her mother and the people around her and who did not speak her language well enough to be able to communicate in it. When they were taking selfies, she even asked him to show her one

DOI: 10.4324/9781003279341-5

of his bracelets – which she observed carefully. She also taught him a few words in Chinese and proudly declared to her mum that she was the 'foreign uncle's Chinese teacher' now. When the 'special session' was over, Fred's friend told him that the little girl had disliked her English lessons and that she had always been quiet and passive with her. But during the 30 minutes of complete chaos in English with Fred, she had memorized more than in the two months that they had been working together. She also noted that she had never seen her being so eager to speak and laugh with an adult stranger – although they could not really 'communicate'. But it did not matter: The little girl had taken control of what she had found 'boring' and, through play and her own agentic moves, she had turned the encounter with Fred into an opportunity to have fun, to laugh and to learn in a different way – while teaching him a few things, from some Chinese words to using a filter on a phone camera. This narrative which had been buried in Fred's memory for years could summarize in itself the main messages of this book.

Unthinking and rethinking *both* children and interculturality

In this book, different and yet complementary ways of examining children and interculturality have been presented by three researchers with a common interest in regularly unthinking and rethinking the thorny notion of interculturality. In each of the chapters one can feel the influence of our slightly different scholarly backgrounds and experiences of working with, teaching about and producing research on children. This is always bound to happen in dealing with interculturality and these multifaceted professional characteristics cannot but enrich the very notion itself in education. One should not forget that our own personal experiences of interculturality are also always there, poking us in the back, influencing us in the way we problematize the notion. While reading the book, our readers might have identified more with and/or disagreed more with some of us; they might also have changed their minds about something and/or reinforced their own views. The same applies to us: in the process of both communicating and writing about the topic of children and interculturality together, we have also managed to renegotiate some of our ways of thinking while confirming some of our beliefs and thoughts. All this will change again in the future – and it should: as a fluid notion, interculturality urges us to watch ourselves constantly and to reimagine it as often as we wish (Dervin, 2022).

In what follows, we summarize what to take away from reading the book, bearing in mind that this is just temporary as problematizing interculturality and children is a never-ending endeavor – no one will ever be able to say: *I am ready now, I know everything about the topic, I know how to 'do' interculturality with and for children, I know a successful formula to introduce interculturality to children,* etc.

As stated in the introduction to the book, we strongly refrain from *imposing* interculturality to children since it goes utterly against the grain of our common understanding of the notion. We would like to reiterate that there are *no ready-made recipes* for introducing children to interculturality, no prefabricated models of intercultural competence that the children can learn gradually as they develop as individuals. We also insist on the fact that the notion of interculturality is always and can never be anything but *polysemous*. This entails that we always have to reinvent our thinking and understanding; constant reflexivity is therefore required when approaching children and interculturality. An idea proposed for achieving this aim in the book is to *interculturalize interculturality* (Dervin & Jacobsson, 2022) by bringing in and allowing different ideas and perspectives about interculturality – even the ones we disagree with – to flourish in research and teach interculturality. Taking children's worlds and perspectives into consideration is, as we see it, an important contribution to our ambition to interculturalize interculturality. As we noted, previous research on children and interculturality often fails to highlight children's perspectives (exception: Piipponen, 2022). Previous research has also focused mostly on one corner of the world (some parts of the West), ignoring other parts of the world such as the Global South – as if interculturality did not take place or mattered for children 'there'. Our book should thus be regarded as an encouragement to move in different directions when working on, about and with children and interculturality. We are just as happy to be criticized for our endeavors and enter into dissensual dialogues on the matter with other scholars, teachers and a generally interested public from different contexts. Without dialogue about research on interculturality and children is as useless as 'to cry wolf'.

While reflecting on the aims of this book, we noticed an interesting aspect that works as a common denominator between the chapters. Regardless of our 'nuanced' reflexivity, the reader will have noticed that, in fact, we regularly *essentialize* the category of children. Fred does this when he describes children as 'the real interculturalists', when Andreas discusses 'childism' in relation to children's culture, and when Heidi suggests activities for antiracist equality. It is also important to note that the fact that we keep reminding our readers about 'children's own perspectives' could be considered as another form of essentialization of children. We are doing this obviously because we find it important to take children's side in the inherent *intergenerational* hierarchical conflict that is always present when researchers focus on children. However, it is important to rethink this issue to engage seriously with the idea of interculturalizing interculturality. Aiming at non- and/or anti-essentialism[1] is commonly highlighted in Western scholarship on interculturality, but as, for example, Aman (2015, 2018) and Dervin and Yuan (2021) have argued and demonstrated, different conceptualizations of interculturality should be based on a continuum moving back and forth between the two unstable poles of essentialism and non-/anti-essentialism. It is therefore important to be aware of this complexity when introducing categories such as *adults, children, culture, ethnicity, race*, etc. These categories might only be stable in relation to a specific context and time but they are as unstable as the notion of interculturality when considered with different lenses.

Children as co-constructors of interculturality – *Placing children's agency at the core*

We have already mentioned several times that we have striven to include children's perspectives in different ways in this book, thereby activating the concept of 'agency'. Agency is one of the most important concepts that have been brought to the forefront by numerous publications in childhood studies, as well as in educational sciences (e.g., Montgomery & Robb, 2018; Prout, 2005; Wells, 2021). To clarify the concept, it can be contrasted with 'socialization' that is used from time to time in educational sciences regarding children and interculturality. The way socialization tends to be problematized is borrowed from the field of social psychology that describes it as the process of being introduced into a socio-cultural community or, in other terms, into a *culture*. The theory of socialization is based on the idea that infants are introduced to a community by being cared for by the immediate family. This is often referred to as *the primary socialization process*, whereby the child encounters and adapts to group behavior, communication and values. What the children learn during this process will eventually be taken over by *a secondary level of socialization*. This happens when the child starts to interact with other people such as friends or teachers, and with different forms of media. Gradually the second socialization is said to take precedence. However, many developmental psychologists (e.g., Sommer, 2005) have criticized these notions, questioning their unidirectionality. According to socialization theory, all influences are *exterior* to the child, merely feeding them with knowledge and behavioral patterns. By presenting the process of becoming part of a 'culture' or a 'community' as a one-way process, socialization is depriving children of their own voice and of their own conscious participation in the creation of their 'worlds' (Sommer, 2005). By highlighting children's agency and their participation in the construction of their own worlds (see the introductory narrative at the beginning of this conclusion) we argue that children's voices are as vital for their cooperation in experiencing and being introduced to interculturality. This critique is also highly relevant

Reflecting on similarities and differences between the chapters

We have now come to the part of our conclusion where we would like to activate the reader in dialoguing with our book. In Table 4.1 we have collected brief extracts from the three chapters that capture some of the main issues that each of us has introduced. The reason for doing this, is to give the reader a 'snapshot' of our different takes and thereby an opportunity to reflect on similarities and differences between how the chapters approach the topic of interculturality and children. We propose that the reader first contemplates the different categories in the table in relation to their own reading of the book: *Do you think that these summaries reflect well the main takeaways from each chapter or did your reading move in other directions?* Secondly, this table can be used for discussing the ideas promoted in the book with others – colleagues, teachers, researchers and perhaps parents – and, at some point, together with children.

Play as a major component of interculturality for children

Although the idea of *play* might sound obvious, with a universally agreed-upon definition, the word is yet another polysemic word in world Englishes and other languages that we need to treat with caution when discussing children and interculturality. Let's take the Chinese language as an example. The equivalent for the word *play* is 玩 (wán). Interestingly, in the Chinese language today, the word is used to refer to any activity beyond professional 'tasks' (work, study) and is not 'just' reserved for children and/or games. As such one might hear some Chinese speakers say in English: *What shall we play this weekend?* (meaning: what shall we do this weekend, beyond work?), *Do you want to play at the mall?* (meaning: let's go to the mall) or *I am glad you found time to play* (to someone who went to a museum). The idea of play thus tends to be reserved to activities that will not lead to productivity, making a profit and ... learning. It is just about relaxing, being happy and putting work aside. Fred remembers how a teacher had rebuked one of her friends when he heard that the friend's son (who was his student) had spent one afternoon 'playing' with a foreigner at an art museum in Shanghai. 'It's a waste of time! He should focus on his textbooks instead,' the teacher said. Fred's friend had argued that this was a great opportunity for her

Table 4.1 Comparing the chapters to reflect on takeaways

Excerpts for comparison	Fred	Andreas	Heidi
Author's intentions	I shall argue that working *on*, and maybe *with*, children and interculturality, requires us to step down from our pedestal as adults and to observe carefully what is happening in children's worlds [note the plural].	...the films that I discuss in the following sections are intended to be watched together with teachers and/or parents to follow up the experience with discussions with the children.	Daycare centers, playgrounds, as well as schools are places for children to experience friendships across races and to meet people from outside their own family circles. In this way children experience interculturality in their lives almost on a daily basis. For education to be more meaningful, I propose a type of early childhood education that recognizes racializing processes and their effects from an early stage as a central part of interculturality.
Three core ideas: 'failure', 'support', 'recognition'	I would like to maintain that the very word 'failure' was chosen for the following reasons: The word tends to be avoided in relation to interculturality since we are often made to think that we should not 'fail' with the other and I have insisted in my work that we must consider failure as an important part of 'doing' interculturality since, I argue, we can learn from failing (Dervin, 2016).	For many scholars with a specific interest in children and childhoods, studying children is not only a research interest, but also a politically and ideologically informed decision to take a stand for and support children.	
Authors' takes on interculturality	*My interculturality is not necessarily your interculturality* and I argue that no one has the right to judge other ways of seeing and 'doing' interculturality, giving too much power to their own take in the process (see Dervin, 2022).	I will also expand on how critical interculturality can be discussed as a topic of general relevance in contemporary societies from global perspectives to prepare for approaching children and interculturality.	In order to problematize children and interculturality, I feel that it is useful and vital to understand how different sociocultural contexts function and the different terms used to discuss interculturality in these contexts, arguing that contexts and curricula affect the way we understand the world.

Conclusion 107

Children's voices	Let us now listen to 15 children whom we interviewed in China about the global world. Choosing Chinese children is important here since their voices are not often heard in global research and in Western media.	To use world cinema is an important and efficient way to introduce children to interculturality and give an insight into the different 'worlds' that children inhabit.	In what follows, I focus on nine Finnish kindergarten teachers who were interviewed and asked to send pictures to describe how they experience interculturality and everyday racism in Finnish kindergartens.
Reactions to previous research and/or ideas on interculturality	My first reaction to what I read was similar to when I read research on university students: researchers tend to start from a preferred ideological take on interculturality ('scientific' but also 'political') when they examine how children behave and/or they discuss intercultural issues.	The general impression is that interculturality is treated as a taken for granted and transparent concept, that is rarely problematized, or for that matter, perceived as necessary to discuss and open up.	Schools can also be an arena for reproducing racist ideas. This might take place in the forms of how curricula, learning materials and educators recognize diversity and questioning the very meaning of diversity.
Characteristics of interculturality and children	After rereading what I have written until now, and to my surprise, I would say that what I found is neither overwhelming nor incomparable to my previous engagement with the field of interculturality in education. The topic is obviously not an easy one and, as I was reading through the literature, I felt sometimes uneasy and started wondering if what some of the researchers were doing was too simplistic in the sense that they seemed to replicate what 'we' have done with adults.	A very important aspect of children's interactions with this type of social media is that a lot of what is produced contains replications of other content. When children produce content, they focus on doing like their peers and often copy what others have already done. From an adult perspective any ideals of authenticity and originality fail to capture children's culture.	Play is vital in (re-)conceptualizing childhood and curricula around the world but it requires sensitivity and preparedness from educators to allow the mixing and socializing that play facilitates to happen. Paramount for intercultural interactions is that the child's experiences and conceptual world are understood and expanded in relationships with other children, educators and learning environments.

son to practice his English while learning new things at a museum. But the teacher disagreed, this was not educational to him, *just play!*

The concept of play has been running as an implicit and explicit red thread in all the three chapters. Play can be considered as the most characteristic concept in all the different fields of study related to children. In early childhood education playing and learning are strongly connected and often considered as children's primary tool for learning. This is particularly true in relation to preschool education in the Nordics (e.g., Johansson & Pramling Samuelsson, 2007). However, play can also work as a way of differentiating children's worlds from adult worlds in other ways, testing out ideas and hypotheses about their world together with their peers (Corsaro, 2017). Play can also be regarded as a liberating space for anarchic and carnivalesque activities where children break the normative rules that adults try to impose on them (Sutton-Smith, 1997; see the introductory narrative to this conclusion).

It is in this final interpretation of play that we can find particular inspiration for further discussions on interculturality and children. To interculturalize interculturality corresponds, to a certain extent, to breaking the rules that are set up by Western academia. We believe that we can find inspiration from children's 'disrespectful' and anarchic ways of playing against the grain, and use Fred's final question from his chapter as a constant reminder: '*How could we remain* children as interculturalists *with our own and shared unstable and contradictory ways when we grow up?*'

Final takeaways for readers

We encourage you the reader to use this book:

- to problematize your own understanding of the notion of interculturality, especially in relation to children, being curious and open to change in the way you see it when dialoguing with others.
- to think further about the notion of children's agency and about your own position in the intergenerational hierarchies that you are involved in either privately or professionally,
- to test, discuss and problematize the empirical material (interviews, films, pedagogical activities) suggested in the book for reflecting on interculturality and children,
- to question adult perspectives on children and interculturality (as Fred puts it: 'to step down from our pedestal as adults').

Let us now play interculturalists together with children!

Note

1 According to Dervin (2022), while 'non-essentialism' represents the *idealistic decision of approaching* the other beyond static representations and stereotypes (among others) in interculturality, 'anti-essentialism' – which he proposed himself in Dervin (2016) – hints at *the awareness of essentialism* while recognizing our incapacity to meet the other without any static representation and stereotype of who we might think they are. Non-essentialism seems to be sold as a miraculous (and yet simplistic and sometimes naïve) solution to 'intercultural problems' at the moment but it must be treated with caution (see discussions in Dervin, 2022; Dervin & Jacobsson, 2022).

References

Aman, R. (2015). Why interculturalidad is not interculturality: Colonial remains and paradoxes in translation between indigenous social movements and supranational bodies. *Cultural Studies, 29*(2), 205–228. https://doi.org/10.1080/09502386.2014.899379

Aman, R. (2018). *Decolonising intercultural education: Colonial differences, the geopolitics of knowledge, and inter-epistemic dialogue.* Routledge.

Corsaro, W. (2017). *The sociology of childhood* (5th ed.). Sage.

Dervin, F. (2016). *Interculturality in education: A theoretical and methodological toolbox.* Palgrave Macmillan. https://doi.org/10.1057/978-1-137-54544-2

Dervin, F. (2022). *Interculturality in fragments: A reflexive approach.* Springer.

Dervin, F., & Jacobsson, A. (2022). *Intercultural communication education: Broken realities and rebellious dreams.* Springer. https://doi.org/10.1007/978-981-19-1589-5

Dervin, F., & R'boul, H. (2022). *Through the looking-glass of interculturality: Autocritiques.* Springer.

Dervin, F., & Yuan, M. (2021). *Revitalizing interculturality in education. Chinese Minzu as a companion.* Routledge.

Johansson, E., & Pramling Samuelsson, I. (2007). *"Att lära är nästan som att leka": Lek och lärande i förskola och skola.* Liber.

Montgomery, H., & Robb, M. (Eds.). (2018). *Children and young people's worlds* (2nd ed.). Policy Press.

Piipponen, O. (2022). *Children encountering each other through stories: Developing a dynamic approach to interculturality in primary schools* (Dissertations in Education, Humanities, and Theology 179) [Dissertation]. The University of Eastern Finland.

Sommer, D. (2005). *Barndomspsykologi: Utveckling i en förändrad värld* (2nd ed.). Liber.

Sutton-Smith, B. (1997). *The ambiguity of play.* Harvard University Press.

Wells. K. (2021). *Childhood in a global perspective* (3rd ed.). Polity Press.

Index

adult-centric 42, 63
adult perspective 3, 4, 63, 64, 67, 69, 70, **107**, 108
agency 5, 6, 48, 49, 52, 64, 66, 104, 108
antiracism 79, 84, 89, 94, 95, 96
audio-visual media 7, 51, 53, 62, 63, 64

childhood studies 5, 6, 52, 60, 61, 62, 64, 104
childism 62, 63, 64, 70, 103
children's culture 63, 64, 70, 103
children's perspectives 62, 63, 64, 66, 67, 69, 70, 103, 104
China 2, 10, 11, 13, 14, 15, 19, 20, 21, 22, 23, 24, 27, 28, 42, 45, 78, **107**
criticality 8, 59
critical race theory 32
critical thinking 35, 36
culture 17, 21, 24, 34, 35, 37, 38, 39, 41, 42, 44, 47, 53, 54, 59, 61, 64, 92, 104
curriculum 34, 36, 37, 38, 56, 76, 77, 79, 80, 81, 82, 89, 90, 91, 95

decolonizing 59
democracy 16, 52, 78, 82
developmental psychology 5, 52, 61, 104
discrimination 31, 76, 82, 91, 94, 96
diversity 4, 6, 7, 33, 34, 37, 40, 41, 43, 45, 55, 58, 61, 76, 79, 82, 86, 87, 88, 89, 92, 94, **107**

early childhood education 5, 6, 7, 41, 51, 67, 76, 77, 78, 79, 81, 82, 83, 84, 88, 89, 90, 93, 95, 97, **106**

equality 22, 62, 64, 76, 77, 80, 81, 82, 95, 103
essentialism 104, 109n1
ethnicity 15, 30, 36, 56, 78, 82, 97n1, 104
Eurocentrism 3, 58, 59, 80, 95

ideological 11, 15, 16, 29, 32, 55, 57, 60, 67, 81
ideology 2, 3, 16, 30, 43, 44, 47, 48, 57, 60, 61
inequality 2, 7, 52, 60, 63, 66, 76
intercultural communication education 2, 43, 54, 56, 57, 61, 62, 67
intercultural communicative competence 2, 3
intercultural competence 4, 38, 47, 56, 57, 58, 59, 103
interculturalist 3, 10, 11, 43, 46, 48, 103, 108
interculturalize interculturality 58, 60, 61, 66, 68, 70, 71n1, 103
inter-epistemology 59, 65, 66
intergenerational 5, 6, 63, 64, 67, 103, 108
internationalization 21, 22, 28, 82

Minzu 15, 21
multiculturalism 83, 90, 91, 94, 32

Nordic 6, 7, 10, 64, 82, 108

othering 56
otherness 17, 32, 59, 67

picture books 32, 33, 35, 36
play 33, 37, 40, 47, 63, 64, 81, 84, 94, 95, 96, 97, 102, 105, **107**, 108

race 15, 17, 31, 32, 42, 44, 47, 76, 77, 78, 79, 82, 89, 92, 93, 95, 97n1
racialization 56, 77
racism 2, 7, 89, 95, 96, 97n1
read-aloud 33, 65

socialization 104
social justice 2, 16, 35, 52, 95

social media 30, 43, 45, 48, 51, 55, 62, 70, 95, **107**
stereotype 44, 46, 67, 68, 109n1

tolerance 16, 32, 45, 48n2, 91

UN Convention of the Rights of the Child (UNCRC) 4, 52, 82
UNESCO 11, 57, 78

Western-centric 10, 42, 59
world cinema 62, 65, 67, 70, **107**

For Product Safety Concerns and Information please contact our EU representative GPSR@taylorandfrancis.com
Taylor & Francis Verlag GmbH, Kaufingerstraße 24, 80331 München, Germany

www.ingramcontent.com/pod-product-compliance
Lightning Source LLC
Chambersburg PA
CBHW070558170426
43201CB00012B/1872